JSON for Beginners: Your Guide to Easily Learn JSON in 7 Days

By iCode Academy

Introduction:

This book contains the steps, strategies, and techniques you need to learn, explore, and use JSON, the preferred and standard data format of the web. It was conceptualized and developed to provide beginners and web developers a comprehensive training that will help them master JSON in as short as one day.

What is JSON and why should you learn it? JSON stands for JavaScript Object Notation. A subset of JavaScript, it is a way of storing information in an organized manner. It provides human readable data that can be accessed easily and logically.

JSON facilitates data transfer between a server and a web application. The JSON format is used to serialize and transmit structured data over the internet. Its simplicity and flexibility allows it to be used across applications, programming languages, and framework.

JSON is a lightweight text-only format that can be easily transferred to and from a server. While it is strongly associated with JavaScript, JSON is a language-independent format that is popularly used in modern programming languages such as Python, PERL, Java, Ruby, and PHP. You'll typically find built-in functions, methods, or workaround that allow these programming languages to utilize JSON.

Using a built-in JavaScript function, you can easily transform a JSON string into a native JavaScript object that can be used like any other JavaScript object in your applications. Other programming languages provide their own functions to convert JSON data to a more usable format.

The emergence of AJAX-powered websites has intensified the need for sites to load data rapidly and asynchronously. The ability to switch contents on the view without requiring total page refresh makes web applications fast, user-friendly, and impressive.

AJAX-enabled sites that rely on RSS feeds from social media sites will run into cross-domain issues if they try to load them with AJAX. JSON provides the method that allows sites to circumvent the single-origin policy. This has opened many possibilities that were previously difficult to navigate. This ability alone makes JSON an extremely useful tool in a developer's kit.

JSON is a faster and less verbose data format alternative to XML. Its grammatical simplicity appeals to many developers and is one of the primary reasons why it has gained acceptance as the internet's standard data format. Developers note the ease of implementing JSON and many acknowledge that it is a more efficient data format than XML.

The advent of Single Page Applications and the widespread and aggressive development of mobile applications resulted in the massive rise to popularity of JSON in 2005 onwards. These modern applications required data interchange to operate quickly and efficiently. JSON provided the ideal format to let them operate seamlessly.

Learning JSON is important if you want to create excellent, fast, and user-friendly web applications. Spending a few hours to study JSON on your own is a worthwhile endeavour that can yield multiple benefits to a web developer.

While it has been around for a while, a beginner will realize that there are too few available resources for fully comprehending and learning JSON. In most cases, it is treated as a sub-study of JavaScript. The json.org website itself is as lightweight and straightforward as its sole subject. Considering that it is an extremely useful data format that has been embraced as a standard in many programming languages and in the dotcom industry itself, it deserves a closer look and a more thorough discussion on its own.

The book "JSON for Beginners: Your Guide to Easily Learn JSON in 24 Hours" provides an intensive, definitive, and practical training to help you discover and apply the many useful and interesting features of this easy-to-learn JavaScript subset as quickly as possible. It seeks to fill the gap in the availability of learning materials that can help beginners comprehend and take full advantage of JSON.

Web developers, absolute beginners, and self-learners will find this book a practical, engaging, and reliable resource material for understanding, creating, and managing JSON data. This comprehensive guide will help you appreciate and optimize the potentials of JSON. It offers a fast, straightforward, and inexpensive way to learn this text-based data exchange format.

JSON is recognized as the standard for data interchange. This suggests that it can be used wherever there is a need to exchange data. Data exchange can occur in many places. It can happen between browser to server, server to browser, server to server, among other means.

With this in mind, this book explores the many ways JSON data can be exchanged. It will help you acquire the skills and confidence you need to utilize JSON in your web applications. You can expect to learn the fundamentals of the JSON format as well as grasp advanced techniques that you can quickly apply in your applications.

While it is used primarily as a data exchange format, JSON data can be optimized to meet your website's requirements. Data persistence is one of the ways to achieve this. The book discusses the basic ways to persist JSON data using cookies and web storage methods. It provides important information to help enhance your understanding of the internet protocol. It features relevant examples and screenshots to help you see JSON in action.

This training will equip you with the best practices used by many web application developers to work with JSON. By the time you finish this book, you will have gained the confidence and technical skills to create, parse, use, post, transmit, and persist JSON.

How long will it take you to learn and master JSON? Most beginners can learn JSON comfortably in 24 hours. If you have strong

HTML and Javascript background, you can easily acquire the important skills in considerably less time. As a self-learner, you have the privilege to decide on the learning pace that will work best for you.

Thank you for downloading this book. May you enjoy learning JSON and may this training help you achieve your career and personal objectives.

CHAPTER 1: THE BASICS

MEET JSON

JavaScript Object Notation, more commonly known as JSON, is an extension or subset of the JavaScript language. It is not, however, a programming language but simply a data interchange format.

While it is used mainly for data exchange between a server and a web application, the JSON format can be used whenever data exchange occurs over the internet.

JSON is a lightweight language independent file format that uses human-readable text to transmit data.

While JSON was derived from JavaScript, there are several other languages that incorporate codes to generate and parse data in JSON format. JSON is routinely used in programming languages like Python, Ruby, Java, PHP, and PERL. This lightweight format is widely used to facilitate asynchronous exchanges between the browser and server.

PREREQUISITES

This book assumes that you have a basic knowledge of JavaScript and web applications' work over HTTP. Some knowledge of object oriented programming will be advantageous.

HISTORY OF JSON

While JSON is widely attributed to Douglas Crockford, a former Atari employee, he himself acknowledged that the more appropriate term was 'discovered' and not 'invented'. He discovered JSON in 2000 while working at State Software.

There were several other people who have discovered independently that JavaScript's object literals can be used as a format to transmit object-oriented data over the internet. Crockford credits a Netscape employee for being the first to apply the idea of using object literals for data interchange sometime in 1996.

Nevertheless, Crockford coined the name JSON, formalized its syntax, and popularized its use for data transfer and storage. He played a key role in the widespread application of JSON alongside the rise of AJAX (Asynchronous JavaScript and XML).

Crockford registered the domain json.org in May 8, 2000 while working as Chief Technological Officer at State Software. He documented JSON's grammar on the site in 2001. He used his high profile status to make JSON a buzzword in the dotcom industry. People noted the ease of its implementation and realized that it is a more efficient alternative to the XML data format.

JSON soared to popularity in 2005 with the widespread development of mobile web apps and the introduction of Single Page Applications. These modern applications required data interchange to operate efficiently and JSON provided the ideal format to let them function seamlessly.

The grammatical simplicity of JSON is one of the primary reasons for its widespread adoption as the internet's standard data format. The same quality makes JSON interoperable and easy to learn.

In July 2006, Crackford standardized JSON'S grammar on RFC 4627 which further defined JSON's composition. Its internet media type is application/json and it is saved with .json as its filename extension.

JSON was formally acknowledged as an ECMA standard with ECMA-404.

JSON VS. XML

A comparison between XML and JSON is inevitable because both are widely used as data interchange format. Depending on what type of data you'll be storing, one format may be better than the other.

- JSON is a concise format while XML is a more expressive or verbose one.
- The repetitive use of tags in XML can be a disadvantage.
- XML is more complex.
- XML uses Xquery specification to query stored XML data. JSON have JSONiq and JAQL although there have been no widespread adoption for both.
- XML has a number of specifications for defining schema or metadata. The list includes XSD and DTD. JSON schema does the same but its use is not as widespread as those of XML schemas.
- A standard specification called XPath is used to select certain parts of XML documents and it is widely used. JSON uses JSONPath but it is not as popular.

JSON is comparable to XML in the following aspects:

- JSON and XML are both human-readable.
- They can be parsed and implemented by a range of programming languages.
- The can be fetched using an XMLHttpRequest.
- They are both hierarchical.

JSON vs. RDMBS

JSON is used to represent or host data. Depending on the structure and type of data you're dealing with, you may prefer to use JSON over RDBMS. This section compares some of the important features of JSON with traditional database models.

- Structure

Relational databases use tables to store data in the form of columns and rows. JSON uses arrays and objects that can be nested recursively. An array is a list of values while and object is a key-value pair.

- Data Retrieval

A relational database uses Structured Query Language (SQL) to fetch data. SQL is a powerful language which is officially recognized as the standard database language. On the other hand, there is currently no widely recognized language that can be used to query the stored data in JSON. Query languages such as JSONiq and JAQL are on the testing stages for this function.

- Sorting

RDBMS data are sorted using SQL. Arrays can be sorted in JSON.

- Metadata

In RDMBS, a schema is used to store information on the type and structure of data that will be stored in the database. Schemas are predefined which means that they are created as soon as you create the database and just before you start storing data.

JSON may also use schema to define the type and structure of data that will be represented. However, the schema, in this case, is not predefined or as restrictive as they are in relational databases. This quality may or may not be an advantage depending on the type of data you'll have to deal with.

- Application

There are several implementations of the SQL and you'll find a good mix of commercial and open-source RDMBS. The most widely used relational database systems include MySQL, Oracle, MS SQL Server, POstgreSQL, and DB2. JSON is commonly used in several programming languages. The NoSQL systems such as MongoDB and CoucheDB use the JSON format to hold data.

- Learning curve

If you're a programmer, you'll find similarities between the structure and basic data types used in JSON and in numerous programming languages. Hence, you'll likely get a grasp of JSON in such a short time. RDMBS is an entirely different field of study.

TYPICAL USES OF JSON

JSON is used to create JavaScript-based web applications that include browser extensions.

It is used by APIs and internet services to provide data for use by internet users.

The JSON format is mainly used for data transmission between a server and a web application. It is used to serialize and transmit structured data over the internet.

Its open format makes it compatible with modern programming languages.

JSON DATA STRUCTURES

The JSON specification supports any of the following data structures:

- collection of key-value pairs
- ordered list of values

collection of key-value pairs

This data structure is widely used among programming languages. It is variably called a dictionary, associative array, keyed list, hash table, record, or object.

ordered list of values

In other programming languages, an ordered list of values is called list, vector, sequence, or array.

The fact that it supports the same data structure used by most modern programming languages makes JSON a highly useful and flexible data exchange format.

CHAPTER 2: JSON SYNTAX

JSON is a subset of JavaScript. Although it doesn't extend JavaScript features, there are subtle differences between JSON syntax and JavaScript syntax. As stated in the ECMA standard 3rd (3rd edition), JSON structures utilize values that are represented by types. It supports four primitive data types and two structured types.

In JSON, a value can only represent a string, object, array, number, true, false, or null. The values true, false, and null must be written in lowercase to avoid generating a parsing error. It is not strictly enforced, but a whitespace can be used before and after a JSON value to make it more readable.

Here is a syntax diagram that illustrates the possible values in JSON:

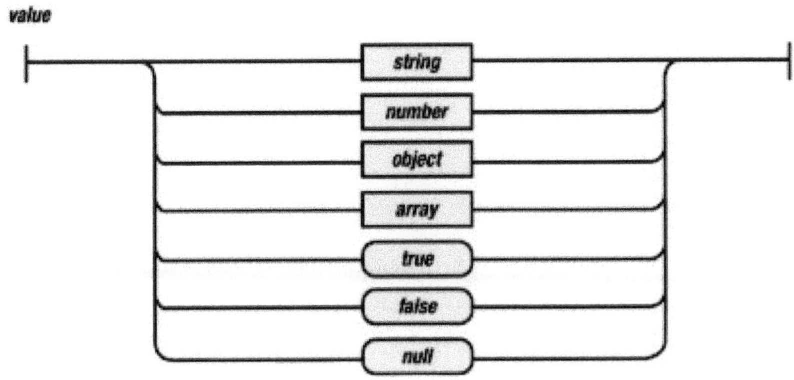

String

In JavaScript, a string can have any number of Unicode characters. They can be enclosed inside a pair of single quotes or double quotes. JSON string, however, should always be written inside double quotes. This helps make JSON interoperable. In C language syntax, for example, a pair of single quotes are used to identify single character like 'a' or 'x' while a pair of double quotes are used to identify a string literal.

Here is a syntax diagram of JSON string value:

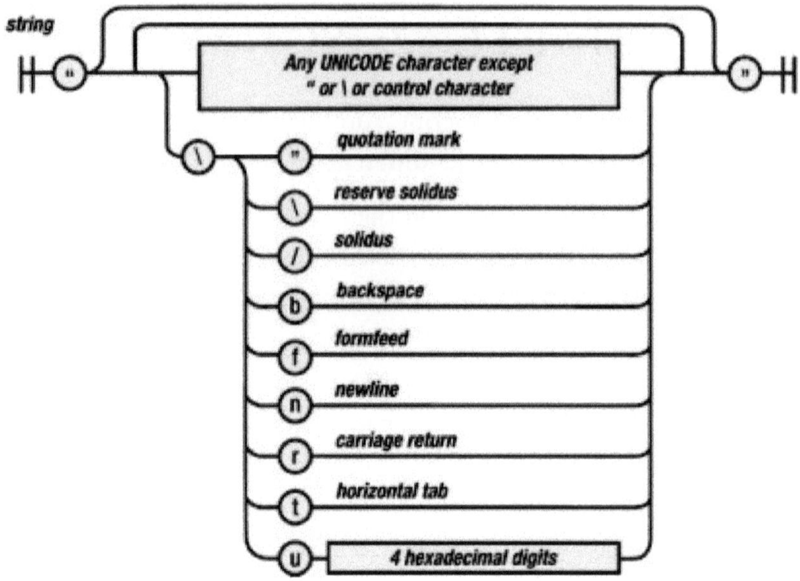

The uppermost path indicates that a string literal may or may not contain a Unicode character.

The middle path indicates that the string can have any Unicode character except for a quotation mark and backlash (solidus).

The second path represents the loops and allows the addition of the outlined characters.

The succeeding paths indicate that a control character can be inserted within the string by escaping it with a solidus (\) character. In addition, the bottom path indicates that you can define a character in its Unicode representation. To specify that a preceding 'u' character is a Unicode value, it must be preceded by a solidus character.

Following are examples of string values:

no Unicode:

"";

Uses backslash before 'u' to denote a Unicode value:

"\u22A0";

Uses escape symbols to display double quotes:

" \" \" ";

random Unicode characters:

" "; "Σ";

Outputs a series of Unicode:

"\u22A0 \" Σ \n";

A backlash or solidus is used to mark characters that have alternate meaning. Escaping characters using a backlash allows us to instruct the lexer to process the character in a different manner. Without it, the lexer can interpret a string as a token and vice versa.

Number

In JSON, a number is the arrangement of base10 literal combined with mathematical notation.

The following diagram illustrates the syntax for numbers:

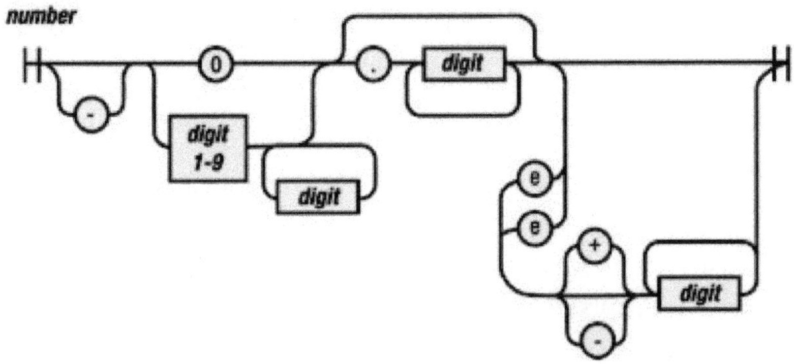

Numbers don't start or end with a symbol the way strings, arrays, or objects do.

A JSON number must comply with the following rules:

A number literal should be positive unless it is explicitly defined as a negative value.

Numbers can't contain superfluous 0's.

Examples:

0.01; -0.01 //valid

00.1 //superfluous, raises a SyntaxError

A number can be in the form of a whole number:

- single BASE10 numeric literal (0-9)
- any number of BASE10 numeric literals (0-9)

A number can be in fractional form:

- base10 numerical literal per placement beyond the decimal
- single base 10 numerical literals at the 10s placement

Examples:
fractional form 1/3
decimal form 0.333333333333333

A JSON number can contain the exponential demarcation literal.

You can express the E notation in either uppercase ("E") or lowercase ("e").

It can be followed immediately by a signed sequence of base10 numeric literals from 0 to 9.

Example:

scientific notation 1.2e-1

Take note that when used within a composite structure, you can use any combination of JSON values as long as you observe proper syntax. The following examples of JSON text contain different types of values:

an array containing primitive values:

```
[
null, false, 4
]
```

an object with two members:

```
{
```

```
"firstname": "William",
"lastname": "Burr",
}
```

an array with nested composites:

```
[
{ "xyz": "134" },
[ "0", 2, 4, 6, 8, 40 ]
]
```

an object with nested composites:

```
{
"object": {
"array": [false]
}
}
```

Chapter Summary

- An object is an unordered collection of name-value pairs.
- An array is a sequential list of values.
- Collections of name-value pairs are enclosed within curly braces {}.
- A member's key should be placed within a pair of double quotes.
- A colon token is used to separate the key from its corresponding value.
- A comma token is used to separate multiple values contained in an array or object.
- The lowercase true/false literals are used to represents Boolean values.
- Successive name-value pairs are separated by a comma (,).
- The double-precision floating point number format is used to

represent numeric values.

- Numbers may be defined with scientific notation.
- The reverse solidus (\) token is used to escape control characters.
- The literal null is used to represent null values.

Chapter 3: DATA TYPES

JSON supports the following data types:

- String
- Number
- Boolean
- Array
- Value
- Object
- whitespace
- null

String

Strings are sequences of Unicode characters enclosed in double quotes with backslash escaping. A character is a string with a length of 1.

Example:

var obj = {name: 'Matthew'}

The following special characters are used with strings:

" double quotation

/ forward slash

n new line

\ backslash

b backspace

t horizontal tab

f form feed

u four hexadecimal digits

r carriage return

Number

JSON supports the integer type, floating-point numeric format, fraction, or exponents.

Example:

{ "age":20 }

It does not use octal and hexadecimals formats as well as infinity.

Array

An array refers to a sequence of values. The elements of an array are enclosed in square brackets and are separated by a comma (,). Indexing can start at either zero (0) or one (1).

Data that uses sequential integers are keys should be contained in an array.

Syntax:

[value, ...]

Example:

{
"employees":["Jackie", "Vincent", "Howard"]
}

Boolean

Boolean values are either true or false.

Syntax

var json-object-name={ string: true/false, ...}

Example:

{ "close":true }

Null

JSON values can be null.

Example:

{"status":null}

Objects

A JSON value can be an object. An object is a set of unordered key-value pairs. Objects are stored within a pair of curly braces {}. A colon is placed between the key and the value. A comma is used to separate key-value pairs. The keys are string data type that must be unique.

The object type is used when the key names contain arbitrary strings.

```
{
"members":{ "name":"Jade", "rating":85, "location":"New York" }
}
```

JSON Key (Name)

The name must be a string inside double quotes. The value can be a string, number, array, Boolean, null, or JSON object. Here's an example:

"name":"Alexa"

Take note that the double quote is required when specifying the key in JSON but not in JavaScript. Additionally, the name always has to be a string, while JavaScript can take other data types such as numerical value or identifier names.

JSON Value

This includes string, number, Boolean, object, array, or null.

Syntax:

Number|String|Array|Object|true|false|null

Example:

```
var x = 5;
var y = "pizza";
var q = true;
```

CHAPTER 4: CREATING JSON OBJECTS

Serialization is the process of converting an object into a form that allows it to be stored or transmitted to a file, database, or memory. The main purpose of serialization is to save the data structure or state of an object in a way that allows it to be recreated when needed. This chapter will discuss the different serialization methods used in JavaScript for JSON.

At the most basic level, the product of serialization is a string. The serialization process involves the construction of the string. The resulting string incorporates the representations of data in their literal form. Capturing data in literal from allows it to be recreated in its original value.

You can convert a JavaScript value into its string equivalent by adding it to another string using the addition (+) operator.

The following examples demonstrate concatenation of primitive values with strings:

```
""+5; //result: "5"
""+false; //result: "false"
""+undefined; //result: "undefined"
""+"Hello"; //result: "Hello"
""+null; //result: "null"
```

While string representations for primitive values can be captured as expected, the use of non-primitive values does not yield the same results as demonstrated by the following examples:

```
""+{identifier:"Hello"}; //output: "[object Object]"
""+["Hello",["hello","world!"]]; //output: "Hello,hello,world!"
```

The above examples demonstrate that while it does have the ability to create objects from literal forms, deconstructing an object to its literal form is not that straightforward in JavaScript language. To accomplish this undertaking, you need to traverse, analyze and assemble the members of an instance into its literal form. This will involve the manipulation of strings, the use of loops, and the proper sequencing of the required structural tokens.

The following table enumerates the different structural character tokens:

Token	Name	Literal
key-value Separator	colon	:
value Separator	comma	,
array opening	left square bracket	[
array closing	right square bracket	]
object opening	left curly bracket	{
object closing	right curly bracket	}

the json object

The json2.js library can be incorporated in an application by referencing the downloaded library inside the <head> tag of an HTML document.

The following example includes the JSON library by creating a reference to its location within the script tag of the HTML document's <head> tag. This example assumes that the json2.file had been downloaded and stored in the js/libs/ folder of the project's working directory:

```
<!doctype html>
<html>
<head>
<meta charset="utf-8">
<link rel="stylesheet" href="css/style.css">
<script src="js/libs/json2.js"></script>
</head>
<body>
</body>
</html>
```

Each time the page is viewed in a browser, the JSON Object defined by json2.js gets added to the global namespace. This allows the serialization method to be accessed anywhere in the scope. While built-in objects like an array or object possesses global methods that can be invoked to create instances of the object using the keyword 'new', the JSON object does not have its own constructor. It does offer two methods: stringify and parse.

the stringify method

The stringify method is used to serialize JavaScript values into a valid JSON object. It takes three parameters: value, replacer, and space.

As discussed earlier, the JSON object lacks the ability to create instances of itself. A simple way to go around this limitation is by accessing the stringify method through the global JSON object.

Here's the syntax:

```
JSON.stringify(value[, replacer [, space]]);
```

The syntax indicates that the value parameter is mandatory while the parameters 'replacer' and 'space' are optional. Although the last two are optional, you'll need to follow the prescribed order of parameters if you need to specify arguments for both. For example, assuming that you want to specify a parameter for 'space' alone, you'll need to provide 'null' as the second parameter.

The value parameter

The 'value' parameter is the only mandatory parameter of the stringify method. It refers to the JavaScript value that you want to serialize. It can be an object, a primitive, or a composite of both. Since arrays and objects are composite structures, the argument for 'value' can contain any nested combination of primitives and objects.

Stringifying a JavaScript Object

To demonstrate the json.stringify method, we'll make use of the following JavaScript object:

var author = { "name":"Jack", "age":27, "location":"Texas"};

To convert the 'author' object into a string, you will use the JavaScript method JSON.stringify() and supply the JavaScript 'author' object as argument:

var myJSON = JSON.stringify(author);

The above statement will produce a string with the JSON notation. Here's the entire code:

```
<!DOCTYPE html>
<html>
<head>
<link rel="stylesheet" href="css/style.css">
<script src-"js/libs/json2.js"></script>
</head>
<body>
<h2>Using the stringify method to create a JSON string from a JavaScript
object.</h2>
<p id-"sample"></p>
<script>
var author - { "name":"Jack", "age":27, "location":"Texas"};
var newOBJ = JSON.stringify(author);
document.getElementById("sample").innerHTML - newOBJ;
</script>
</body>
</html>
```

This will be the result:

Using the stringify method to create a JSON string from a JavaScript object.

{"name":"Jack","age":27,"location":"Texas"}

Stringifying a JavaScript Array

You can also use the stringify method to convert JavaScript arrays into a JSON string.

To demonstrate, here's a JavaScript array:

var emp = ["Dylan", "Nicole", "John", "Ashley"];

To convert the array into a JSON string, use the stringify method and supply the emp array as argument:

var myOBJ = JSON.stringify(emp);

The statement will produce a JSON string.

Here's the code:

```
<!DOCTYPE html>
<html>
<head>
<link rel="stylesheet" href="css/style.css">
<script src="js/libs/json2.js"></script>
</head>
<body>
<h2>Creating a JSON string from a JavaScript array.</h2>
<p id="sample"></p>
<script>
var emp = [ "Dylan", "Nicole", "John", "Ashley" ];
var myOBJ = JSON.stringify(emp);
document.getElementById("sample").innerHTML = myOBJ;
</script>
</body>
</html>
```

The code will produce the following result:

Creating a JSON string from a JavaScript array.

["Dylan","Nicole","John","Ashley"]

The following example converts nested objects to a JSON string using the stringify method:

```
<!doctype html>
<html>
<head>
    <meta charset="utf-8">
    <link rel="stylesheet" href="css/style.css">
    <script src="js/libs/json2.js"></script>
</head>
<body>
    <script>
    //obtain reference to the body tag
    var body = document.getElementsByTagName("body")[0];
    //function log appends a value to the body for output
    function log(jsonText) {
        //supplies jsonText with double quotes, appends a new line
       body.innerHTML += '"' + jsonText + '"<br>';
    }
    var employee = new Object();
        employee.name = "Jack";
        employee.age = 27;
        employee.children = [
            { name : "Robert" , age : 4.5 },
            { name : "William" , age : 2 }
        ];
        var JSONtext = JSON.stringify(employee)
        log( JSONtext );
    </script>
</body>
</html>
```

The stringify method returns the following JSON text:

"{"name":"Jack","age":27,"children":[{"name":"Robert","age":4.5},{"name":"William","age":2}]}"

Notice the precision in which the string output was captured from the data stored within the employee object.

Take note that the serialization process is a synchronous one. This means that once the stringify method is invoked, the remaining code will have to wait for the completion of the process before it can be executed. Hence, it's a smart idea to keep the objects as concise as possible during the process.

The preceding examples showed how powerful and useful the serialization process can be. You have so far seen it at work with values that are considered valid within the JSON syntax. In real life, an application's requirements can become more complex and you may encounter unexpected results using the same process.

While you can expect a program written in JavaScript to utilize most, if not all, of the language's features, you should bear in mind that JSON is a subset of JavaScript. As such, a great number of the primitives and objects used in your application may be serialized in a different, often unexpected, way. It's important to understand how the stringify method handles particular values so you can anticipate the serializer's output.

The stringify method does not recognize some types of values.

The serializer handles an undefined value in two different ways. If the undefined value is found within a property, it removes the entire property from the JSON string. If the undefined value is found in an ordered list, it is converted to 'null'.

The stringify method analyzes and encodes values but doesn't evaluate them. It disregards functions, including those that return a string to the key that holds the function. When it encounters a function, the stringify method will convert it to the undefined value. The rules on undefined value as described in the preceding paragraph will apply to the key that references the undefined primitive.

In the following example, the stringify method is used to convert a list of key-value pairs to a string literal. One of the key-value pairs uses a function to return a value:

```
<!DOCTYPE html>
<html>
<head>
<link rel="stylesheet" href="css/style.css">
<script src="js/libs/json2.js"></script>
</head>
<body>
<h2>The stringify method removes functions from an object.</h2>
<p id="sample"></p>
<script>
var author = { "name":"Jack", "age":function () {return 27;}, "location":"Texas
"};
var myOBJ = JSON.stringify(author);
document.getElementById("sample").innerHTML = myOBJ;
</script>
</body>
</html>
```

Here's the result:

The stringify method removes functions from an object.

{"name":"Jack","location":"Texas "}

Notice that the stringify method removed both the 'key' ('age) and 'value' from the JSON string.

You can work around this limitation by converting the function into a string literal before serializing the object. For example, if you want to retain the function in the above example, you can run the following statement before invoking the stringify method:

```
obj.age = obj.age.toString();
```

To demonstrate, the following example converts the function to a string literal before serializing the list of key-value pairs:

```
<!DOCTYPE html>
<html>
<head>
<link rel="stylesheet" href="css/style.css">
<script src="js/libs/json2.js"></script>
</head>
<body>
<h2>The stringify method removes functions from an object.</h2>
<p>To keep the function, convert it into a string object before serializing.
</p>
<p id="sample"></p>
<script>
var author = { "name":"Jack", "age":function () {return 30;},
"location":"Texas"};
author.age = author.age.toString();
var myOBJ = JSON.stringify(author);
document.getElementById("sample").innerHTML = myOBJ;
</script>
</body>
</html>
```

Here's the result:

The stringify method removes functions from an object.

To keep the function, convert it into a string object before serializing.

{"name":"Jack","age":"function () {return 30;}","location":"Texas"}

As much as possible, you should refrain from using functions in JSON. Functions lose their scope in JSON and you'll need to invoke the eval() function to deserialize them.

Since JavaScript does not have a date literal, the serializer automatically converts dates into JSON string literals with the ISO encoding format.

In the following example, the stringify method is used to convert a list of key-value pairs where one of the values is the current date:

```
<!DOCTYPE html>
<html>
<head>
<link rel="stylesheet" href="css/style.css">
<script src="js/libs/json2.js"></script>
</head>
<body>
<h2>The stringify method converts date objects into string literals.</h2>
<p id="sample"></p>
<script>
var author = { "name":"Jack", "today":new Date(), "location":"Texas"};
var myOBJ = JSON.stringify(author);
document.getElementById("sample").innerHTML = myOBJ;
</script>
</body>
</html>
```

It will produce the following result:

The stringify method converts date objects into string literals.

{"name":"Jack","today":"2017-07-26T19:39:18.860Z","location":"Texas"}

Number values should be finite. If evaluated as infinite or NaN, the number will be returned as a literal 'null' value.

The following example uses the stringify method to serialize a value that evaluates to infinity:

```
<!DOCTYPE html>
<html>
<head>
<link rel="stylesheet" href="css/style.css">
<script src="js/libs/json2.js"></script>
</head>
<body>
<h2>The stringify method returns null when a number is infinite .</h2>
<p id="sample"></p>
<script>
var myOBJ = JSON.stringify(1/0);
document.getElementById("sample").innerHTML = myOBJ;
</script>
</body>
</html>
```

Here's the output:

The stringify method returns null when a number is infinite.

null

When the only value serialized is a string value, the stringify method escapes and nests the literal form inside another set of quotes.

JSON can't manage cyclic object values. This means that an object or array cannot possess a value that refers to itself. Attempting to define a cyclic structure will immediately generate an error.

toJSON

You have learned earlier that date objects don't have a literal form. Hence, when the stringify method is used to serialize a date value, it converts the date into a string literal. You might assume that this is produced by invoking the toString method of the date object. The Date.toString() method, however, does not generate a standardized output. Instead, it produces a string representation with a format that varies with the browser's locale.

Because this output lacks a standard, it's not ideal to serialize it for data interchange. A more logical solution would be to convert the content into the ISO 8601 grammar.

You can use this feature by calling the toJSON method which is included in the Crockford library. This method should be appended to the date object's prototype for it to be inherited by all date objects. The following example shows the default toJSON function that will exist on any dates:

```
Date.prototype.toJSON = function(key) {
function f(n) {
// Format integers to contain at least two digits.
return n < 10 ? '0' + n : n;
}
return this.getUTCFullYear() + '-' +
f(this.getUTCMonth() + 1) + '-' +
f(this.getUTCDate()) + 'T' +
f(this.getUTCHours()) + ':' +
f(this.getUTCMinutes()) + ':' +
f(this.getUTCSeconds()) + 'Z';
};
```

Whenever the stringify method calls the toJSON method, it has to provide a return value. In the above example, it provides a string as the return value. The string is formed by concatenating the method attributes of the instance being analyzed. The result can be any value specified in the subset.

The stringify method proceeds to analyze the value. It does so in an iterative manner if the value is returned as an object. More simply, when the value returned is a primitive one, the stringify method sanitizes the value after converting it into a string.

The above example also invokes the f() function. Its purpose is to wrap each method and add a 0 prefix to the result if the returned value is less than 10. This is required to maintain the fixed number of digits.

The function f wraps each method and prefixes each result with 0, if the returned number is less than 10, in order to maintain a fixed number of digits.

Each number is placed in a logical sequence along with different tokens and assembled into a string. This results to a valid grammar that conforms to the ISO 8601 specification.

The toJSON method may likewise be used for values or purposes other than dates. Assuming that an object possesses the toJSON method, the stringify method's internal logic invokes the toJSON method when it analyzes the object. This indicates that toJSON can be added to a built-in JavaScript object or to a custom class where it can be inherited by its instances. When the toJSON function is attached to the object, it becomes available to all JavaScript objects. Likewise, you can add the toJSON method to individual instances.

The object's inherent ability to add the toJSON method allows the application to supply the required encoding.

Whenever the toJSON method is called, a key is provided as an argument. This is used to reference the key of the value currently being analyzed by the stringify() method.

If the key is an array's index, the argument given should be an index. If the key is an object's property, the property label is assigned as the key of the method. The latter will give a good insight when one is devising a conditional logic based on the context of the instances while the former is less indicative.

replacer

Replacer, the second parameter in the stringify method, is optional. Once provided, it will modify the default behavior of the serialization process.

The method allows two forms of argument for 'replacer'. You can supply a function that modifies the way arrays and objects are serialized or an array of numbers and strings that provides a list that you can use to select the properties of the object that you want to serialize.

replacer Array

To demonstrate the use of an array as argument for 'replacer', assume that you have the JavaScript data structure shown below:

```
var emp = new Object();
emp.name="Johann";
emp.age=29;
emp.email="johann@yawn.com";
```

To serialize the structure using the JSON object and its stringify method, you can provide the 'emp' instance as the value with this statement:

```
JSON.stringify( emp );
// "{"name":"Johann","age":29,"email":"johann@yawn.com"}"
```

Assuming further that the e-mail addresses are not supposed to be serialized by the application, you can easily remove the e-mail property by passing the emp object through the stringify method. While this will easily solve the problem at hand, it may prove difficult if the application require the e-mail address at some future time. Instead of deleting the e-mail value, you can use the replacer method.

The process can be as simple as providing the replace parameter with an array of values that reflect the attributes that you want to serialize. The following example includes an array that specifies the properties (name and age) that you want the application to serialize:

```
JSON.stringify(emp, ["name","age"]); // "{"
name":"Johann","age":29"}"
```

The ordered list supplied as replacer argument is used as the basis for filtering the properties that will be generated during serialization. Identifiers that are not defined inside the replacer array will not form part of the JSON string. Additionally, the order of the specified properties determines the order of their appearance in the serialized output. For example, the following statement will produce a JSON object containing the same properties as the above example but in a different order:

```
JSON.stringify(emp, ["age","name"]); // "
{"age":29","name":"Johann"}"
```

The attributes specified in the replacer array will be displayed in the JSON text in the order in which they appear in the array. Hence, in the statement, the 'age' will be shown before the 'name'. You can attribute this to the fact that an array is an ordered list.

replacer Function

Instead of providing a replacer area, you may want to supply a replacer function. Providing a function as a replacer argument lets the application insert the logic required to determine the processes involved in the serialization of objects inside the stringify method.

The replacer function can be compared to the toJSON method and the two are almost identical except for some features. For one, the replacer function is a function while the other is a method. The replacer function is supplied in an iterative manner. Lastly, the replacer function has access to the value associated with the key.

Here's the syntax for the replacerFunction:

```
var replacerFunction = function( k, v );
```

Based on this syntax, you'll notice that the replacer function requires two arguments. The 'k' argument represents the key or the identifier of the object that the method wants to serialize. The 'v' argument stands for the value of the 'key'. Take note that when you use the replacer method with an object that holds a toJSON method, the 'v' argument will be equal to the output supplied by the toJSON method.

To demonstrate, the following code logs all keys, values, and context using the replacer() function:

```
var emp = new Object();
emp.name = "Jack";
emp.age = 27;
author.pets = [
{ name : "Robert" , age : 4.5 },
{ name : "William" , age : 2 }
];
JSON.stringify(author,
function(k,v){
console.log(this);
console.log(k);
console.log(v);
return v;
});
```

space

The third parameter in the stringify method is space and like the replacer, it is also optional. The space argument lets you define the amount of padding that will separate the values from one another inside the JSON object. The use of padding adds readability to the output string.

The argument given to the space parameter should be a whole number which is equal to or greater than 1. Any number less than 1 will be ignored and will have no impact on the output string. The values in the JSON object will be indented with the given value of whitespace from the left margin.

You can establish a margin by including new line character after the {,} and [, and] tokens. The new line-control characters are added to the JSON object after the opening and closing tokens for both object and array. In addition, a new line character is provided after a separator token.

The following example compares the output string with and without padding:

```
var obj={ primitive:"string", array:["x","y"] };
JSON.stringify(obj,null,0);
// (no padding)
// "{"primitive":"string","array":["x","y"]}"
JSON.stringify(obj,null,6);
/* (6 spaces of added padding)
{
array: [
x,
y
]
}"
*/
```

The supplied argument on the space parameter will not take effect on the JSON string if it doesn't have an object or array. In the following example, the supplied argument indicated that six spaces must be added to the JSON text. Since it does not possess an array or object, the given padding was not applied:

```
var primitive="string";
var JSONtext=JSON.stringify( primitive , null ,6 );
console.log( JSONtext );
// ""string""
```

Take note that the padding added to the produced JSON text will have no effect when it is converted back into a JavaScript object. In addition, including new line characters and white space does not have a significant effect in its internet transmission speed.

Chapter Summary

- Numbers should be finite. Otherwise, they will be treated as null.
- A value that does not qualify as a valid JSON value outputs an undefined value.

- Properties with undefined values are stripped.
- An undefined value in an array is regarded as null.
- The primitive null is processed as a null string.
- A cyclic structure raises a TypeError Exception.
- The toJSON method and the replacer argument allow an application to provide the logic required for serialization.
- A replacer array is used to identify properties that must be serialized.
- A replacer function can be called with any property in the data structure.

CHAPTER 5: PARSING JSON

Parsing is the process of analyzing something in conformity with established rules. Parsing can be applied in natural or computer languages.

Because JSON grammar is a subset of JavaScript, the parser analyzes its token in the same manner that the JavaScript Engine parses source code. Hence, the analysis of JSON grammar will produce data in the form of arrays, objects, numbers, and strings. It also generates the literals true, false, and null. You can refer to these data structures like any other JavaScript value in your programs.

In this chapter, you will learn the different ways of converting a valid JSON object into a JavaScript value that can be utilized in your programs.

JSON.PARSE

In the previous chapter, you have learned to create a JSON object from JavaScript objects using the stringify method. There is another method that works in the opposite direction: the parse method. The parse method is used to convert serialized JSON into usable JavaScript values. In addition to its availability through the browsers that are compliant with the ECMA 5th edition standards, the parse method can be accessed from the json2.js library.

Here's the syntax for the parse method:

```
JSON.parse(text [, reviver]);
```

Based on the given syntax, the parse method takes two arguments: text and reviver. The text parameter name indicates the value it expects to receive. The reviver parameter provides the ability to enable custom logic to be provided for required parsing that would not have been possible by default. The text argument is mandatory while the reviver argument is optional.

The text parameter indicates the type of JavaScript value that must be provided: a string. More specifically, it requires serialized JSON. This requirement is important because an invalid argument automatically produces a parse error.

For example, the following invalid JSON grammar throws a Syntax Error:

```
var str = JSON.parse( "123xyz" ); //SyntaxError: JSON.parse: unexpected character
```

The example threw a syntax error because a string literal was provided, not a serialized JSON. You will recall that in the previous chapter, you have learned that when the sole value of a string is serialized, the literal value is wrapped inside an additional pair of quotation marks. Hence, the string "123xyz" should be escaped and captured inside an additional set of quotes.

The following example shows a valid string value that was successfully parsed:

```
var str = JSON.parse( "\"123xyz\"" ); //valid JSON string
value
console.log(str) // 123xyz;
console.log(typeof str) // string
```

Once a JSON text is parsed, the resulting JavaScript value is returned to method's caller to allow it to be assigned to an identifier. This will make the JavaScript value accessible throughout the program.

The above example used a simple JSON string but it might as well have been a composite such as an ordered list or a collection of key-value pairs. When the JSON text is a nested data structure, the converted JavaScript value will retain all nested elements.

the eval function

The eval function is a global object's property. It takes a string as an argument. The string can represent a statement, expression, or both and is evaluated as JavaScript code.

In the following example, the eval function is used to evaluate a string as JavaScript code:

```
eval("alert(\"Hello, World\")");
```

The above example transforms the string "Hello, World" into a JavaScript code. The string which represents a statement is also evaluated as a statement. Ideally, you'll see the text "Hello, World" when you run the program. However, this may not always happen. You should always be cautious of the argument that you provide to the eval function.

The following example will demonstrate how the eval function is used to evaluate expressions:

```
var answer = eval("2+12");
console.log(answer) // 14;
```

The preceding example demonstrates that you can also use the eval function to return the output of an evaluated expression. This allows the expression to be assigned to a variable which can be accessed in an application.

If you were to provide the eval function with a sting that references an object literal, the argument will likewise be evaluated as an expression. The string will be returned as a JavaScript instance corresponding to the object literal it represents.

Here's an example:

```
var array = eval("['Winnie','Minnie','Daisy']");
console.log(array[1]) //Minnie;
```

It is important to ensure that the provided text is a sequence that conforms to valid JSON grammar. Neglecting to do so can cause malicious code to be injected into the application. While it has the ability to handle the conversion of JSON into a JavaScript value, you must avoid using the eval() function directly. You should use the JSON2.js library or take advantage of the built-in JSON object on browsers.

THE PARSE METHOD

A close scrutiny of the json2.js library will reveal that the parse method works through four stages to perform its function.

In the first stage, the parse method ensures that characters are appropriately escaped. This averts syntax errors caused by the treatment of Unicode characters as line terminators. The following example demonstrates that a string with a carriage return or line breaks should not be submitted for evaluation:

```
var note="this sentence contains a new line
... this is the new line";
// SyntaxError: unterminated string literal
// Similarly
eval("\"this sentence contains a new line\u000a... this is
the new line\"");
// SyntaxError: unterminated string literal
```

The SyntaxError message indicates that the string literal containing a line break was interpreted as an unterminated string literal.

Section 7.3 of EMCA-262, however, allows the use of escaped line terminator character inside a string literal token. By placing an escape sequence before specific Unicode values, you can use a line break inside string literals and submit it for evaluation. The following example shows how this can be accomplished:

```
eval("\"this sentence contains a new line\\u000a... this is
the new line\""); //valid statement
```

In the second stage, the parse method uses regular expressions to ensure the validity of grammar. The method aims to locate tokens that do not conform to valid JSON grammar. In particular, it attempts to find JavaScript tokens that could potentially harm the application. These tokens include the following:

- method invocations which are indicated by open and close parenthesis ()
- left-handed assignments which are signified by the equal operator which can be used to modify current values
- object creation denoted by the 'new' keyword

While it explicitly searches for the above tokens, the parse method will raise a syntax error and cease evaluating the text when it finds invalid tokens. If the text appears to be valid, the method will proceed to the next stage.

In the third stage, the parser will supply the sanitized text to the eval() function. At this time, the captured literals of JSON values are ideally converted to their original form. Remember, however, that JSON grammar does not allow several JavaScript values including methods, functions, dates, custom objects, nonfinite numbers, and undefined literal. In such cases, the text will be reconstructed to as close as possible but not precisely into their original form.

The parse method allows you to further scrutinize the output JavaScript values in the final stage. During this stage, you can control what JavaScript values can be returned and used by your program. If you fail, however, to supply an argument for the reviver, the parser will simply return the JavaScript value generated by the eval() function.

The fourth and final stage will occur only if a reviver argument was supplied to the method. The inclusion of this optional parameter will enable you to supply the logic required to control the JavaScript values that will be returned to the program. This will not be possible if you will only rely on default behavior.

The reviver argument

Unlike the replacer argument of the stringify method, you can only supply a reviver parameter through a function.

Here is the syntax for the reviver parameter:

```
var reviver = function(k,v);
```

The statement indicates that the reviver function takes two arguments which will help determine how the JavaScript values will be returned. The first argument refers to the index or key of the value for evaluation. The second argument corresponds to the value associated with the index or key named in the first argument.

When you supply a reviver function, the JavaScript value produced using the global eval method is traversed iteratively. The loop will seek the current object's properties and probe deeper into nested structures it may possess as values. When a value is evaluated as a composite object (array or object), its corresponding key is likewise iterated over. The process will continue until all enumerable key-value pairs are uncovered. The JavaScript engine controls the order by which the properties are traversed.

The scope of the reviver function is constantly aligned to the context of the object possessing the key-value pairs provided as argument. This means that when an object supplies its properties as arguments, it will stay as the context of the implicit 'this' inside the reviver() function.

Lastly, the reviver method needs to return a value each time it is invoked. Otherwise, it will return an undefined JavaScript value.

The example below indicates that members will be deleted if the reviver returns an undefined value:

```
var JSONtext='{"name":"Johann","age":29,"children":
[{"name":"Robert","age":4.5},{"name":"William","age":2}]}';
var reviver= function(k,v){};
var employee = JSON.parse( JSONtext,reviver);
console.log(employee) //undefined
console.log(typeof employee) //undefined
```

By this time, you're well aware that JSON captures dates as a string of the UTC ISO format. This prevents the eval() function from handling the conversion of this string into a JavaScript date. You may, however, work around this limitation. If you can determine, for instance, that the value provided to the reviver function is a string in UTC ISO format, you can instantiate a date, provide it with the ISO-formatted string literal, and return a JavaScript date to your program.

The following example transforms an ISO date-formatted string into a date object using the reviver function:

```
var date= new Date("August 1 2017");
var stringifiedData = JSON.stringify( date );
console.log( stringifiedData ); // "2017-08-01T05:00:00.000Z"
var dateReviver=function(k,v){
return new Date(v);
} var revivedDate =
JSON.parse( stringifiedData
, dateReviver);
console.log( revivedDate ); //Date {Tue Aug 01 2017 00:00:00 GMT-0500 (EST)}
```

The reviver function which contains the required logic enabled the parser to return a JavaScript date to the program. A reviver function almost always has to possess the required conditional logic to control when and how to evaluate the value provided. String values provided to a reviver function can be tested against ISO 8601 grammar. If the string is compliant, it is converted into a date.

Chapter Summary

The parse method is the mechanism used to convert a JSON text into a JavaScript value. By adding the json2.js library to an application, you can make this method available to both modern and older browsers.

To convert captured literals, json2.js uses the eval function to access the JavaScript engine. The eval function is a built-in global function. While using this function can cause nefarious code to be inserted into an application, the risk is minimized by searching for non-matching patterns in the provided text against JSON grammar. A parse error is thrown when it encounters tokens that appear to instantiate, modify, or operate. Additionally, finding such tokens causes the parse method to exit which prevents the submission of the potentially harmful text to the eval function.

If the text supplied is considered appropriate for eval, the captured literals will be processed and converted into JavaScript values. However, objects such as custom classes or dates cannot be transformed natively. In such cases, the parse method can use an optional function to manually modify the JavaScript values to suit the format required by an application.

The use of clearly defined label keys in the toJSON, reviver, and replacer functions will enable an application to efficiently control the revival of serialized data.

- The parse method throws a parse error if a JSON text does not comply with JSON grammar.
- The eval() is not a secure function.
- Only valid JSON should be supplied to eval.
- A reviver function can be used to return valid JavaScript value.
- If the reviver returns an undefined value for a member, that member is removed.
- If the reviver returns the argument provided for the value parameter, the current member is unchanged.
- The reviver is used to manipulate JavaScript values.

CHAPTER 6: JSON DATA PERSISTENCE

Earlier, you learned how the JSON.stringify method is used to capture the data or state of a JavaScript value and transform it into a JSON text. In addition, you learned further that the JSON parse method relies on the JavaScript engine's natural ability to parse the literals of a JSON text. The process revives a previous model's state and allows it to be used in the current session.

While the stringify and parse methods were illustrated one after the other in the previously examples, it is not typical in real life to parse data as soon as it was serialized. These methods, however, can be paired with data persistence to allow them to work independently of each other.

Data persistence is defined as a continuance of a state after the process that created it has terminated.

The serialization process ends as soon as a JSON text is generated and the function that implemented the process has terminated. To be able to utilize the JSON text produced by the process, it must be stored properly.

One of the internet technologies that you can use to achieve data persistence of JSON is that of HTTP cookie.

HTTP COOKIE

The HTTP cookie was created for the purpose of stringing together the requests of an internet user and facilitating the persistence of the state of a page into another. A cookie is a packet of data set by a website and retained by your browser. The browser subsequently supplies the retained cookie to the server upon request.

With JavaScript, a cookie can be used on the client side of web applications. In addition, as it is provided inside the header of every browser request, the server has access to the cookie. The header can then be parsed to make the cookie available to server-side script.

Cookies enable back-end and front-end technologies to work together and replicate the captured state. This allows the proper handling of requests or page views and causes isolated actions to occur within the user's interaction with a website.

Cookies have their own protocol and specification. You can take advantage of the persistence of the cookie by learning and understanding its syntax and using that knowledge to persist JSON for subsequent use.

A cookie, in its basic form, is a sequence of ASCII characters. ASCII stands for "American Standard Code for Information Interchange". It consist of 128 characters from the English alphabet, basic punctuation, some control characters, and the digits 0-9.

The following outlines the full syntax of the HTTP cookie:

```
cookie = NAME "=" VALUE *(";" cookie-av)
```

The above statement specifies the following:

Set a cookie specified by the NAME to the assigned VALUE.

Based on this, you can deduce that a cookie is simply a key-value pair. Like other key-value pairs, the key or in the case of cookies, the NAME, is used as an identification and a means to access the corresponding value. The VALUE, in this case, refers to the state or data that you want to persist.

To make sure that cookies are stored in a uniform manner across browsers, both the NAME and VALUE should contain valid ASCII characters.

Here are examples:

```
"message=Hello World!";
"messageJSON=[\"Hello World!\"]";
```

While the JSON text is made up of tokens with valid ASCII characters, it can contain values such as UTF-8. If your application contains values other than those in the ASCII RANGE, You will need to encode the UTF-8 values using Base64 encoding.

For this purpose, you can use any of these two libraries:

https://code.google.com/p/javascriptbase64/

https://jsbase64.codeplex.com/releases/view/89265

Going back to the cookie syntax, the second half, *(";" cookie-av) states that you can provide the cookie with a series of optional attribute-value pairs which must be separated by a semicolon (;). Providing a whitespace between pairs is not mandatory but will help keep the code clean and readable. Possible cookie-av value can be one of the following: "expires", "path", "domain", "max-age", "httponly", and "secure". An attribute value specifies a scope to a defined cookie.

The expires attribute

This attribute specifies the duration of persistence of a given cookie. If specified, the value tells the browser up to what time and date it should store the cookie. The value should conform to the UTC GMT format. Since this is a standard, you can easily achieve this by using the Date object's built-in methods.

The following example uses the toUTCstring method to generate a UTC GMT value:

```
var date= new Date("Aug 1 2017 12:00 AM");
var UTCdate= date.toUTCString() ;
console.log( UTCdate ); // "Tue, 01 Aug 2017 06:00:00 GMT"
```

When the date's built-in method toUTCstring was used on the specified date string, the time and date was converted to its GMT equivalent and subsequently returned to the method's caller. The abbreviation GMT which was appended to the logged value indicates that the date had been converted.

If you will assign the date on the above example to the 'emp' cookie in the next example, that would make the cookie available until Tuesday, 12 AM August 1, 2017 or Tuesday, 01 Aug 2017, 06:00:00 Greenwich Mean Time.

The following script appends Data to the Key-Value Pair and specifies expiration to the cookie:

```
var date= new Date("Aug 1 2017 12:00 AM");
"emp=test; expires="+ date.toUTCString();
```

By default, the cookie will persist as long as the session is open. Hence, if you omit the value for the 'expires' attribute, the cookie is purged from memory as soon as the session has ended. If you provide a past date as the value of the 'expires' property, the cookie would be discarded immediately.

In the past, you can expect all sessions to close as soon as you exit the browser. Nowadays, it's not uncommon for sessions to persist long after the browser had been closed. This is usually attributed to features supplied by vendors to their browsers. One example is the browser's ability to restore previously viewed pages in the event that the browser crashes or is halted due to an unexpected event. This feature also enables us to restore tabs or pages from the browser's History log. Hence, session cookies may persist in memory longer than usual.

You will want to supply a value to an 'expires' attribute for your cookies if you wish to persist JSON indefinitely.

max-age

Like the 'expires' attribute, the 'max-age' attribute defines the life span of a cookie. The difference is that in 'max-age', the duration is expressed in seconds. While this attribute still exists today, it is not recognized by IE 6 to 8. Hence, the 'expires' attribute is referred over the 'max-age' attribute.

The Domain Attribute

To set a cookie, you'll use the domain attribute to define the domain(s) to which the cookie will be accessible. When specifying the domain, you should bear in mind that it should be related to the domain which sets the cookie. For example, if the domain www.myforum.com is setting a cookie, it can't define www.yourblog.com as the domain.

It's the browser's job to make cookies available to the server and JavaScript. Before it can do that, the browser must first compare the cookie's supplied domain attribute against the domain of the visited URL and ensure that the domains match.

The following regular expression illustrates the comparison:

```
var regExp=
(/www.myforum.com$/i).test('www.myforum.com');
```

The example illustrates a pattern that matches the host domain. The use of the $ token explicitly declares that the pattern ends with '.com' and forces a tail end match. This is important because you would want to prevent the cookies of www.myforum.com from being accessed by another domain that may contain the originating domain name in its subdomain.

For example, myforum.xyz is an entirely different domain from xyz.com. Assuming that xyz.com had opted to use the subdomain myforum.xyz.com, here's what may happen if you try to match the two URLs:

```
(/myforum.xyz/i).test('myforum.xyz.com'); //true
(/myforum.xyz$/i).test('myforum.xyz.com'); //false
```

The example demonstrates that the omission of the $ token as shown on the first line can potentially result in two different properties being evaluated as a match. The use of the $ token on the second line forces a tail-end match where the matching was performed on the top level domain.

Once the browser has established a match between the server domain and domain attribute, it will send all cookies to the server and make it available to the JavaScript application.

The 'i' specifies that the match should be case-insensitive.

While the domain attribute is not required, you may want to set it for security purposes. When not set, the default value for the domain property will be the cookie's originating domain. Relying on the default value may limit the advantages of using cookies. For instance, a subdomain that requires the visibility of cookies will not have access to the cookies if the domain attribute has been set to its default value, the top level domain level.

Assigning a domain attribute value allows you to broaden the cookie's scope. The use of the '.' token before the top-level domain will make the cookies accessible not just to the top-level domain but to the subdomains as well.

The following chart illustrates which origins will match the value of the domain attribute:

Origin	Domain Attribute	Result
myforum.com	www.myforum.com	false
www.myforum.com	myforum.com	false
myforum.com	.myforum.com	true
www.myforum.com	.myforum.com	true
health.myforum.com	.myforum.com	true

The path attribute

The path attribute sets the subdirectories where a cookie will be made available. If not set, the default value is the directory where the cookie was set. In addition, all subdirectories of the default directory will be given access to the cookie.

Setting the path attribute, however, confers some advantages. You can broaden or narrow the scope of the cookie to a specific directory and its subdirectories by defining the path.

The secure attribute

The secure attribute ensures that the cookie is transmitted by the browser only within a secure connection or HTTPS. Sending cookies over a secure connection lessens the possibility of having their content viewed by network hijackers while in transit. The word secure, however, may be slightly misleading because it does not protect the cookie against an attacker who may attempt to overwrite or delete the cookie.

The httponly attribute

When specified, the 'httponly' flag makes the cookie available to the server alone. It effectively prevents client-side JavaScript from accessing, updating, or deleting the cookie. When used in combination with the 'secure' attribute, it reduces to a large extent the possibility of exploiting the cookie through cross-site scripting. Take note that only the server can set the httponly flag on cookies. Since your objective is to persist JSON data on the client-side, you should not use this attribute.

document.cookie

There are different ways to create a cookie. The server, HTML meta tags, server-side scope, and JavaScript can be used to build a cookie. This chapter focuses on creating and retrieving cookies through JavaScript. In reality, a cookie only becomes a cookie when it is supplied to the document.

The document object in JavaScript can be used to reference the DOM (Document Object Model). This object comes with a range of interfaces that will allow you to manipulate HTML elements and others. The document.cookie interface is one of those interfaces.

The document object's cookie attribute supplies the browser with a given string of key-value pairs which enables the persistence of these key-value pairs. In addition, the cookie property provides the necessary interface for their retrieval.

The following example uses the document.cookie property to create a cookie:

```
document.cookie="myFirstCookie=xyz123";
```

The use of the equal = sign or assignment operator may create an impression that a string is being assigned to the document's cookie property. In reality, the string is being supplied as a parameter to a setter method, an internal method that handles changes made to a variable. The method takes each assignment as a value and stores it in an internal collection, also called the cookie jar.

The collection is stored in a file which is only accessible to the browser that stored it. As each browser sets the cookies in its own cookie jar, the cookies are only accessible to the specific browser which was open when they were set.

Since no value is actually being assigned to the document.cookie property, you can add as many key-value pairs as you want to the document.cookie without overwriting previous settings.

The following lines illustrate subsequent assignments to document.cookie:

```
document.cookie="myFirstCookie=xyz123";
document.cookie="mySecondCookie=egbdf";
document.cookie="myThirdCookie=doremi";
```

Subsequent assignment to document.cookie does not override the previous key-value pair assignment as key-value pairs are not treated as value and are instead stored inside the cookie jar. The cookie jar is located on the computer's file system. It is a resource which gives cookies the ability to persist.

Viewing and Managing Cookies

Depending on your browser, here are the different ways to view and manage all cookies on your computer:

Chrome:

Open Chrome navigate to chrome://settings

At the end of the page, click 'Advanced'.

Under 'Privacy and Security', click 'Content Settings'.

Select 'cookies'.

Navigate to 'All cookies and site data'.

To view individual cookies, click on the show more button on the right. To delete the cookie, select X. To remove all cookies, select 'Remove All'.

Firefox:

On the menu bar, Select' Options' and Click 'Privacy'.

Under History, choose 'Use custom settings for history'. To manage the settings, check or uncheck the boxes for each setting. To view the cookies, click 'Show Cookies'. To delete a cookie, mark the cookie and click 'Remove Selected'. To remove all cookies, click 'Remove All'.

While it has many uses, cookies have limitations. A cookie can only store up to 4 kilobyte of data or about 4,000 ASCII characters. The amount may seem large enough for average requirements but that will depend on what you intend to store. Since the document.cookie only provides information on the stored key-value pair, there's no way to find out how many bytes are still available.

In addition, cookies are scoped to the browser. This means that it is only accessible to the browser that preserves it.

In terms of data persistence, the cookie is considered archaic by today's standards. HTML5 introduced the Web Storage to address the limitations of the cookie in client-side data persistence.

WEB STORAGE

HTML 5 did not necessarily create the Web Storage tool to replace the cookie. The cookie performs a vital role in maintaining the session between the server and the browser while Web Storage exists to fill the limitations of the cookie in client-side data persistence.

Web Storage provides a much larger amount of storage than what the cookie can offer. Its maximum capacity per origin is about 5MB.

Much like the cookie, the Web Storage API allows the state to be stored using JavaScript either for the session's duration or indefinitely.

Web Storage, like its predecessor, focuses itself on the persistence of key-value pairs. As the value that must be provided to the storage object has to be in string form, JSON data is the logical choice for handling what would otherwise be cumbersome data.

JavaScript can access Web Storage through the WindowObject as Window.sessionStorage and Window.localStorage. As the window object is global and accessible from any scope, you can shorten the reference to sessionStorage and localStorage.

While both objects allow the storage of state using the same API, they differ in the duration of data state retention. The sessionStorage object lets data persist until the end of the session. On the other hand, the localStorage allows data to persist indefinitely until the state is removed by the user through the browser or by the application.

Web Storage Interface

Web Storage allows the storage, retrieval, and removal of data through its API.

Following are the components of the Web Storage API:

Components	Parameter
setItem	string (key), string (value)
getItem	string (key) string (value)
key	Number (index)
removeItem	string (key)
key	Number (index)
length	
clear	clear

setItem

The setItem of the Storage object is the method used to persist data. Web Storage, like the cookie, retains data in key-value pairs and distinguishes the key from its value. Hence, setItem requires two string arguments: the name of the key and the value to be held.

Syntax:

setItem(key , value)

When a value has been set successfully, the method will not provide a response to the caller. However, if the value was not set as expected, it will throw an error. This can occur if the storage capacity has been reached or if the user had disabled the storage.

To prevent your script from terminating due to runtime error, you must wrap your call to the setItem within a try/catch block.

The following statement stores myFirstItem:

```
localStorage.setItem("myFirstItem,"xyz123");
```

Like JavaScipt object key-value pairs, each key must be unique. If you try to store a value to an existing key name, the existing value will be overwritten by the new value.

Hence, if you want to replace an existing value for a key, you can use setItem to set the new key-value pair.

Example:

```
localStorage.setItem("myFirstItem,"xyz123");
localStorage.setItem("myFirstItem,"123abc");
```

If you will try to retrieve the current value of myFirstItem at this point, you'll get "123abc".

getItem

The getItem method of the storage object is used to retrieve the persisted state/data corresponding to the specified key.

Syntax:

getItem(key)

The following statements attempt to obtain a value for a given key:

```
console.log( localStorage.getItem( "myFirstItem" ) );
//123abc
console.log( localStorage.getItem( "mySecondItem"
) ); //null
```

Specifying the key as argument to the getItem() method will return the value for the given key. If the key does not exist, the method will return a null value.

removeItem

The removeItem method is the only way to actively end the persistence of a key-value pair. It takes only one argument: the key of the data that you no longer want to retain.

syntax:

removeItem(key)

The following statements use the removeItem to cause a persisted state to expire:

```
console.log( localStorage.getItem( "myFirstItem"
)); // 123abc
localStorage.removeItem( "myFirstItem" );
console.log( localStorage.getItem( "myFirstItem"
)); // null
```

clear

The clear method is used to instantly purge all key-value pairs. It does not require an argument.

syntax:

clear( )

key

The key method is used to retrieve the identities of stored keys that contain the accompanying data stored by the Storage Object. This method will take an index and return the value of the index. If the specified index does not have a value, it will return a 'null' value.

syntax:

key(index)

length

The length property is used to access the length of values retained by the Storage Object. This is useful when you want to provide indices within the boundaries of stored keys. You can achieve this by using the length attribute with a loop as demonstrated by the following code:

```
var maxIndex= localStorage.length;
for(var i =0; i<maxIndex; i++){
var foundKey = localStorage.key( i );
}
```

Chapter Summary

- Data persistence is the continuance of a state after the process that created it has terminated.
- Cookies are sent with every HTTP/1.1 request.
- Web storage and cookies are used to retain state.
- Session data will cease to exist after the session exits.
- Sessions do not necessarily end when a browser is closed.
- Cookies are exchanged through HTTP and/or HTTPS.
- Cookies can only contain 4KB of ASCII characters.
- Cookies can be shared among subdomains.
- Web Storage can store 5MB of data.
- Each origin has its own Storage Object.
- Web Storage strictly implements the same-origin policy.

CHAPTER 7: DATA INTERCHANGE

You have learned so far to work with JSON data within applications. JSON is first and foremost a data interchange format which is capable of being transmitted over the internet. This ability can be used to provide more possibilities to your applications.

The use of data interchange allows the transmission of JSON over the internet into a target database. The data could be sent with the HTTP cookie and web storage which protects it from being deleted easily by site visitors. The ability to transmit data offers far more benefits than allowing you to load the stored data into an application. It also enables you to access the data that others may be willing to share either for free or through a paid service. The most common examples are social sites that allow the public to access the data they have captured. The many useful attributes of JSON makes it the preferred data format of almost all social API.

At this point, it will be useful to understand the communication that transpires during a resource request and the server's response.

HTTP

The Hypertext Transfer Protocol, more commonly known as HTTP, is the underlying mechanism that facilitates interactions with the internet. It is used along with underlying networks of protocols to enable the request/response between the client and the server.

The client used in the request or response process can be a web browser like Internet Explorer, Firefox, or Chrome. It can also be a client of another server. Whichever way, the request/response can only occur if a request was initiated and a response can only come from a server. A request should be initiated whenever a resource such as a document, style sheet, or image is requested from the server.

HTTP REQUEST

The request provides the details of the required resource. These specifics help ensure that the server will provide the required response.

The HTTP request is made up of three general components each of which has specific uses.

Following are the parts of a Request:

Request Line

Headers

Entity Body

Of the three components, only the Request Line is mandatory.

Request Line

The Request Line handles the type and resource of the request as well as the version of the HTTP protocol being used by the client. It consists of three parts which are separated by whitespace: Method, Request-URI, and HTTP-Version.

The method specifies the action that will be performed on the given resource. It can be any of these keywords: GET, POST, DELETE, LINK, UNLINK, TRACE, HEAD, PUT, and OPTIONS.

The GET method tells the server that it possesses a resource that you want to obtain. It is most commonly used when you're navigating to a specific URL. This method is generally regarded as a safe method because it is not concerned with any modifications to a server.

The POST method tells the server that you will be sending data with your request. It is typically used with HTML forms. This method is commonly considered an unsafe method because it involves data modification.

The request line's URI identifies the resource that the request method utilizes. The URI may be a dynamic script in which the content is generated at the time of request. It can also be a static resource like a CSS file.

The Request Line should specify the HTTP version used by the client. From 1990 onwards, the Request-Version has been HTTP/1.1.

Following are examples of a Request Line:

```
GET
http://health.myforum.com/chapter3/css/style.css HTTP/1.1
GET
http://health.myforum.com/chapter3/img/dog.jpg HTTP/1.1
POST http://health.myforum.com/chapter3/post.php HTTP/1.1
```

Headers

The header component of the Request tells the manner used by the Request to supply supplemental meta data. This data is provided within in header form. At its most basic level, a header is a key-value pair separated by a colon (:) and consists of ASCII characters. This data helps the server to determine the best response to the Request.

The HTTP protocol offers numerous headers that can be used to send various types of data to a server. The headers can be one of the following types: general, request, or entity headers.

General Headers

A general header is used to identify general information about the request. It may include the date of request and other useful information such as whether or not the request should be cached.

The following are examples of general headers:

Date

Connection

Cache-Control

Warning

Via

Pragma

Transfer-Encoding
Trailer
Upgrade

Request Headers

The Request can include Request Headers which contain information that can be used by the server to handle the request. These headers provide an outline of the requesting client's configuration or the data type that a response must generate. The use of request headers allows you to influence the server's response.

Below is a list of Request headers:

Accept
Accept-Encoding
Accept-Language
Accept-Charset
Referer
Range
User-Agent
Host
From
Proxy-Authorization
Max-Forwards
Expect
Authorization
If-Modified-Since
If-Match
If-Unmodified-Since
If-Range
If-None-Match
TE

The Accept header, in particular, is highly useful. You can use it to tell the server the data type or MIME type that can be handled properly by the client. It can be set to a specific MIME type like text/plain or application/json. You can set it to */* which tells the server to process all MIME types.

Entity Headers

The entity headers supply additional information about the resource found in the body of the HTTP request, also called entity body. They convey the data required by the server to access and present the entity, including its data type, content length, character encoding, and number of data bytes.

These are entity headers:

Content-Type
Content-Range
Content-Location
Content-Length
Content-MD5
Content-Languages
Content-Encoding
Allow
Expires
Last-Modified

Entity Body

The entity body is the name given to the data transferred in the form of a request or response. Its syntax may reflect XML, HTML, or that of JSON. If the Content-Type entity header is not provided in a request, the server will need to predict the data's MIME type.

HTTP RESPONSE

An HTTP Response refers to the message that a server transfers to a client machine in response to its HTTP Request. The HTTP/1.1 protocol provides the following structure for an HTTP response:

```
status-line
header-line
...
header-line

entity-body
```

The HTTP Response structure has three parts: status line, header line, and entity body. Notice that expect for the status-line, it contains basically the same parts as the HTTP request.

Of the three parts, only the status-line is mandatory in a Response. A Response can have zero to several header lines which can come in any order. It can only have zero or a single entity-body. The status line, header line(s), and blank line should end with CRLF characters ("/r/n"). A blank line separates the header lines and entity-body.

Below is an HTTP Response with two header lines:

```
HTTP/1.1 200 OK
Content-Type: text/html
Content-Length: 39

<html><body>Hello, World!</body></html>
```

Status Line

The status line of the HTTP Response provides information on the result of the request.

Example:

HTTP/ 1.1 200 OK

The status line consists of three parts: the HTTP protocol version used, a status code, and a description of the status related to the numeric status code. A whitespace separates the parts from one another.

The status code is a three-digit number that corresponds to the status of the request. There are five groups of statutes each which can contain up to 100 unique status codes.

Status Code	Description
100-199	This class of status code indicates a provisional response, consisting only of the status line and optional headers.
200-299	This class of status code indicates that the client's request was successfully received, understood, and accepted.
300-399	This class of status code indicates that further action needs to be taken by the user-agent, in order to fulfill the request.
400-499	This class of status code is intended for cases in which the client seems to have erred.
500-599	This class of status code indicates cases in which the server is aware that it has erred or is incapable of performing the request.

Front-end developers more commonly encounter the following status codes:

200 OK

The server has received and fulfilled the request.

204 No Content

The server has received request but there is no entity body to return.

404 Page Not Found

The server is unable to locate the specified resource.

500 Internal Server Error

The server has encountered an issue which prevents it from fulfilling the request.

Headers

The response header provides a mechanism which enables the server to provide the client with meta information along with the response. Response headers, like request headers, have three categories, namely request headers, general headers, and entity headers.

General Headers

The general headers provide general information regarding the response. Here are the general headers:

Date
Connection
Cache-Control
Warning
Pragma
Transfer-Encoding
Via
Upgrade
Trailer

Response Headers

The response headers supply the requesting client with data on the server's configuration and the requested URI. Here are the response headers:

Server
Age
ETag
Accept-Ranges
Location
Retry-After
Proxy-Authentication
WWW-Authenticate

Vary

Entity Headers

The entity headers provide meta information on the data transferred with the response. The most useful entity headers are those that describe the entity's MIME type which allows it to be read or parsed properly. The Content-Type header is used for this purpose.

Below are the Entity headers:

Content-Type

Content-Encoding

Content-Range

Content-MD5

Content-Location

Content-Length

Content-Languages

Last-Modified

Allow

Expires

Entity Body

The entity body refers to the data transferred by the server.

AJAX

Asynchronous JavaScript and XML, also known as AJAX, is the method of communicating to and from a server and updating sections of a web page without having to completely refresh the page. AJAX provides the ability to initiate HTTP Requests on demand without the need to leave the current page.

AJAX has powered modern front-end development and although the X stands for XML, requests or responses initiated through AJAX are still bound to the HTTP protocol. Hence, the server can transfer valid data types including XML, Text, HTML, and JSON. Originally though, the XMLHttpRequest only supported parsing with XML.

JavaScript uses the XMLHttpRequest object to initiate an HTTP Request within an executing application which enables the client to communicate asynchronously with the server. This allows the user and the running application to continue working without having to pause or wait until the server had fulfilled the request.

XMLHttpRequest Interface

The HTTP API is a set of various properties, methods, states, and event handlers which enables a JavaScript application to successfully send an HTTP request and obtain a response from the server. Hence, each property, method, state, and event handler is essential in specific aspects of the request or response.

Global Aspects

The constructor is the only global method of the XMLHttpRequest interface. When called, it returns a new instance of the XMLHttpRequest object to the application. The interface inherited by this object can be used to initiate and handle requests. In addition, instantiating multiple instance of this object will enable handling of simultaneous requests.

The following statement creates an instance of the XMLHttpRequesr Object:

```
var xhr = new XMLHttpRequest();
```

The example instantiates an XMLHttpRequest objects and assign the value to the xhr variable.

Since the HTTP request happens asynchronously regardless of the number of xhr you may be working with, the application needs to be notified of changes in state while the request is being processed. These will include notifications on whether the connection has timed out or when the request has been fulfilled. Each instance of xhr possesses event handles which allow you to monitor the status of the HTTP request.

Below is a list of xhr event handlers:

Event Handlers	Event Type
onprogress	progress
onreadystatechange	readystatechange
onabort	abort
ontimeout	timeout
onloadstart	loadstart
onloadend	loadended
onload	load
onerror	error

The Request Aspect

The request methods and properties of the xhr object allow you to configure the metadata of the request.

Below are the four methods of the xhr object:

- open
- setRequestHeader
- send
- abort

The open method

The open method is the starting point for the configuration of the HTTP request. It has the following signature:

```
open( HTTP-Method, request-URI [, async [, user [,
password]]]);
```

Based on its syntax, the open method takes five arguments of which two are mandatory and three are optional.

The HTTP-Method parameter tells the server the method should be implemented on the request URI.

The request-URI parameter names the target of the request. The argument can be defined as either absolute or relative URL. Take note that the URI supplied should match the origin of the application seeking to configure the request. If the URL supplied belongs to a host other than the current origin, the targeted URL's server should allow resource sharing for cross-origin.

The third parameter, an optional one, indicates whether the request should occur synchronously or asynchronously. If omitted, the default value is 'true' which causes the request to be processed in another thread.

The user and password are optional argument that can be used to provide resource credentials when basic authentication is required for access. The values supplied will only be added to the HTTP request metadata if the server throws the status code 401 Unauthorized.

The setRequestHeader method

This method allows the application to specify headers by supplying additional information to complement the request. The supplemental data can be one of the attribute-value fields of HTTP.1.1.

Here's the syntax for this method:

```
setRequestHeader( field, value );
```

The statement indicates that the field and the value should be provided as individual strings. The xhr object appends the arguments together and uses the colon token to separate them. You can provide any number of request headers to a request.

The setRequestHeader method allows the application to provide any attribute value that will help the server fulfill the required response. The Accept headers provide the media types that the application recognizes.

You can also provider headers to represent attribute values that can be used to support custom request. By convention, custom headers are preceded by X.

The following example uses the setRequestHeader method to provide an accept header and a customer header:

```
setRequestHeader( "Accept", "application/json" );
//requesting JSON as the response
setRequestHeader( "X-Custom-Attribute", "Pick-a-Prize"
); //custom header
```

While you can provide most HTTP/1.1 headers, there are a few headers that can't be overridden to protect data integrity and security. Below are the headers that can't be set through JavaScript:

Accept-Charset	Cookie
Accept-Encoding	Cookie2
Access-Control-Request-Headers	Date
Access-Control-Request-Method	DNT
Connection	Host
Content-Length	Expect
Transfer-Encoding	Origin
Keep-Alive	Referrer
User-Agent	Upgrade
Trailer	TE
Via	

The send method

The send method is used to indicate the submission of the request.

Here's the syntax for the send method:

```
send( data );
```

The send method can be called with an argument. The argument supplied corresponds to the entity body of the HTTP request. It is commonly used when the request method indicated is potentially unsafe like the POST method.

The argument should be provided in string format. It can be a word or a list of key-value pairs.

The abort method

This method tells the HTTP request to cancel or discontinue the request. It prevents the client from establishing a connection with the server or closes the connection.

The Request Properties of the xhr Object

The xhr object provides some attributes that can help you configure the request.

Here are the properties:

Properties Returned Value

Timeout Number (duration)

upload XMLHttpRequestUpload (object)

withCredentials Boolean (credentials)

The timeout property is implemented by all modern browsers and IE 8. The upload and withCredentials properties require IE 10 or higher.

timeout

The timeout attribute is used to set the duration of the time required to complete the request. It can start from milliseconds to any numeric value. The supplied value will be the maximum time allowed for the server to process the request. The timeout event is dispatched to notify the application when the request surpasses the allotted time.

upload

The upload attribute gives the application a reference to the XMLHttpRequestUpload object. The object enables the application to monitor the transmission progress of a specified request. This can be useful for an entity-body which contains a large amount of data as in the case of applications that allow users to upload file attachments such as videos or images.

withCredentials

The value of the withCredentials attribute can be set to true or false. In cross-origin resource request, the value is used to tell the server that credentials have been provided.

The Response Aspect of the xhr Object

The xhr object provides methods and attributes that are used to work with the headers of the HTTP response.

Earlier, you have learned that the HTTP request and response have three matching components: request-line/status-line, headers, and payload. The payload and headers are combined to form a parsed response. However, they are obtained individually using the xhr interface.

Here are the response methods of the xhr interface:

Method	Parameters	Returned Value
getAllResponseHeaders	N/A	String(value)
overrideMimeType	String(Content-Type)	N/A
getResponseHeader	String(value)	String(value)

The getAllResponseHeaders method

This method is used to return all headers sent by the server along with the response. When called, the xhr object returns a string in key-value pairs which are separated from each other by new line control characters and carriage return. Additionally, the colon token is used to separate the key from its value.

You can parse the returned string and extract the headers into an array using string manipulation techniques.

getResponseHeader

This method can be used to fetch the value for the response header as set by the server. This method provides metadata that can be useful in coordinating how the data supplied can be displayed, updated, or utilized.

Here's the syntax of the getResponseHeader method:

```
getResponseHeader( key );
```

Take note that if the key provided is not a server-configured header, the method will return the null value. The argument must be a string which can be in uppercase or lowercase.

If the key supplied is not a configured header among those possessed by the response, the value returned will be that of null. Much like getAllResponseHeaders, being able to analyze the meta-information supplied within the response can be vital in coordinating how you display, update, or even utilize the data provided.

overrideMimeType

This method allows the application to override the Content-Type of the response body as configured by the server. Modern browsers are implementing this method.

Obtaining the HTTP Response

The following attributes of the xhr object enables us to obtain the response to the HTTP request:

Properties	Access type	Returned Value
readyState	Read	Integer (state)
responseType	Read/ Write	XMLHttpRequestResponseType (object)
status	Read	Integer (HTTP status Code)
statusText	Read	string (HTTP status)
responseText	Read	string (value)
responseXML	Read	XML (value)
response	Read	* (value)

readyState

This property displays the present state of the HTTP request. This attribute is continuously being updated to reflect the current status of the request.

status

This attribute enables the application to fetch the status code of the response. There are five categories of status codes which were discussed earlier.

statusText

This attribute is used to fetch the textual phrase associated with the HTTP status code. For instance, the 200 is a status code that comes with the textual phrase 'OK'. This property allows the application to relay a more descriptive report to the user. This is also helpful when debugging.

responseXML

This attribute allows the application to fetch an XML response supplied by the server. The responseXML property may not provide a value if the data provided in the response is not configured as XML Content-Type, text/xml, or application/xml. If a server provides a response for a data with a non-XML Content-Type, this will be returned as 'null' when read within the application.

Take note that responseXML is not limited to XML documents. You can also use it to fetch HTML documents of text/html Content-Type.

responseText

This attributes enables the application to fetch the raw text of the entity body. Unlike responseXML, responseText will always return a value. Since the responseText property supplies the application with the raw entity body in string format, you have to obtain the Content-Type header value as well. This will provide information on the syntax required to parse the string. Once this is accomplished, you can parse the string into the desired format.

responseType

This attribute deals with the parsing of data types natively beyond XML. The xhr object possess the ability to parse a response into XML data but since XML is not the interchange standard today, much of the parsing had to occur on the client side which places the responsibility on the application. This heightens the risk of blocking the JavaScript engine's single thread. Allowing the browser to perform the parsing job reduces the possibility of blocking JavaScript's thread.

Specifying the responseType property on the request causes the entity body to be parsed using the indicated syntax. The following example specifies JSON syntax for parsing:

```
var xhr = new XMLHttpRequest();
xhr.open("POST",
"http://mysite.com/chapter5/quiz.php");
xhr.setRequestHeader("Content-Type", "application/json");
xhr.setRequestHeader("Accept", "application/json");
xhr.onreadystatechange = changeInState;
xhr.responseType = "json";
xhr.send('{"fname":"Joshua","lname":"King"}');
```

response

The xhr object's response attribute allows the application to fetch the entity body of the request that had been fulfilled by the server. Unlike the responseText and responseXML, the value returned will be parsed if the HTTP request had been set to responseType. Otherwise, it will return an empty string.

The following example sets the request to use the responseType:

```
var xhr = new XMLHttpRequest();
xhr.open("POST", "http://mysite.com/chapter5/quiz.php");
xhr.setRequestHeader("Content-Type",
application/json);
xhr.setRequestHeader("Accept", "application/json");
xhr.onreadystatechange = changeInState;
xhr.responseType = "json";
xhr.send('{"fname":"Joshua","lname":"King"}');

function changeInState() {
var data;
if (this.readyState === 4 && this.status === 200) {
var mime = this.getResponseHeader("contenttype").
toLowerCase();
if (mime.indexOf('json'))) {
data = this.response;
} else if (mime.indexOf('xml'))) {
      data = this.responseXML;
}
         }
      }
}
```

Setting the request to responseType causes parsing to be performed as a separate action. This means that you no longer have to parse JSON within the application. Instead, you can utilize the response property which, at this point, is holding a JavaScript object.

Chapter Summary

- A client initiates the request.
- Only a web server can provide a response.
- General headers refer to general information.
- Request headers transmit preferential data.
- Entity headers provide useful information about the provided entity body.
- Entity headers and general headers can be set by both server and client.
- Response status code indicates the status of the request.
- The Accept header indicates the data types it can work with.
- The XMLHttpRequest object facilitates JavaScript HTTP request..
- The server recognizes the .json extension and takes on application/json as the Content-Type.
- Custom headers start with X.
- Status code 200 means the request was sent successfully.

CHAPTER 8: CROSS-ORIGIN RESOURCES

The XMLHttpRequest object provides front-developers a simple way to interchange data using JavaScript. In the past, a sequence of full-page requests had to be performed to facilitate data exchange. The advent of AJAX made it possible to create HTTP request within JavaScript.

While it has injected dynamism to web pages, the prevalence of AJAX exposed websites to risks of being injected with nefarious code. This is a serious concern for websites that transmit data and even more so when it involves critical data such as bank accounts, credit cards, or personal identification.

To minimize a site's exposure to malicious requests, the XMLHttpRequest can be set to grant network access only to resources that are deemed trustworthy.

In this chapter, you will learn about same-origin policy (SOP) and its impact on the resource interchange between two different origins.

SAME-ORIGIN POLICY

Same-origin policy or SOP has been in use ever since JavaScript was introduced. To this day, it remains a vital aspect of web security. User-agents commonly adhere to SOP as a security model.

The SOP controls a good number of front-end securities including those that surround cookies, DOM access, network access, and web storage. It can be applied to web plug-in such as Silverlight, Java and Flash.

In previous examples, you have seen how the HTTP request was utilized to POST data on the specified resource. When a request has been received successfully, the server would respond by way of providing an entity body. Take note that the user-agent generally does not permit this behavior. You may have to employ techniques for that specific resource to allow Ajax request to succeed.

The browser's user-agent generally won't permit the request to push through for the reason that the origin used to initiate the request does not match the origin of the resource. The SOP, in general, places a limit on the network message that one can send to another. It prevents a resource from one origin to obtain the resource supplied by another origin to prevent the injection of malicious content.

The SOP is implemented by user-agents that are being utilized to make network requests. Take note that for legacy purposes, SOP policies might differ in the level of enforcement between web technologies.

A resource is deemed authorized to retrieve or obtain content from another resource only if it possess exactly the same port, domain, and scheme as the other resource.

This is the syntax of an HTTP URL:

```
scheme://domain:port/path/?key=value
```

The port is not always required in the URL but accounted for like the other components of the URL.

Scheme

The scheme or protocol specifies how the given resource will be obtained. It can be specified as http, https, or ftp.

The typical scheme used by most web sites is 'http'. However, the scheme can also be 'https' where 's' indicates that the transmission is secure. The https is commonly used by banks or online stores but Google is currently exerting pressures for other sites to use https as well.

Domain

The domain is a human-friendly way to refer to a specific location in the internet. Behind the scenes, the domain name is converted to a static IP address.

Port

The port number is used to specify an application which is being run on a common IP address. It's an optional end point. If not defined, the default port for the given scheme is used. The HTTP scheme uses 80 as its default port. On the other hand, the HTTPS scheme uses 443 as its default port.

The user-agent uses the three aspects of the HTTP-URL to decide if it should enforce the SOP.

As an added protection and to prevent a script from forging the request, some headers are not allowed to be defined though the setRequestHeader method of the XMLHttpRequest object. These headers are explicitly defined by the user-agent. Attempts to supply a value for these headers through the setRequestHeader will be overridden by the user-agent.

Here are the headers:

Host

Origin

Via

Referer

Browsers are called user-agent because they work on behalf of the user. The user-agents implement the SOP to ensure safety in internet interactions. It's extremely important to grasp the concept of SOP and the functions of user-agents if you're planning to utilize network access for exchanging JSON data. While back-end programming has the ability to bypass SOP limitations, front-end developers have user-agents working for them.

WORKING AROUND SAME-ORIGIN POLICY

As mentioned earlier, the browsers restrict network access that occurs between two different origins for the purpose of implementing the same-origin policy. There are, however, some loopholes that front developers can exploit to allow cross-origin requests.

CORS

Cross-Origin Resource Sharing (CORS) is one of the techniques that you can use to side step the SOP. CORS is the mechanism approved by W3c for handling cross-origin requests. While it does not disable or remove SOP, CORS works by enabling a server to allow requests that don't qualify as trusted. In turn, this tells the user-agent to allow the response to be served from varying origins.

During the request, the server and user-agent use special HTTP headers to communicate with each other and determine if the request should be processed.

The Access-Control-Allow-Origin is only one among nine headers defined by CORS. The user-agent can set three of these headers to accompany the request while the server can configure six headers on the response. Not all of these headers are required to authorize an HTTP-Request. A maximum of four is exchanged in most cases.

The number and type of headers required to authorize a request will depend on whether the request is considered "simple" or one that requires "preflight". Ultimately, a request is categorized as simple or preflight based on the request method specified to act on the given resource and the request headers used.

Simple Requests

A simple request specifies POST, GET, or HEAD as its request method. In addition, it can only specify the following headers:

Content-Type

Content-Language

Accept

Accept-Language

A simple cross-origin communications begins when a client makes a POST, GET, or HEAD request on the server.

In a basic scenario, the request will include an Origin header which identifies the client code's origin. A POST request can only have one of the following content type: text/plain, multipart/formdata, or application/x-www-form-urlencoded.

The server evaluates the Origin of the request and determines if the request should be allowed or disallowed. If the request is allowed, the server will respond with the requested resource. The response will include an Access-Control-Allow-Origin header. The special header indicates the client origin that will be given access to the resource. The browser will permit the request if the Origin of the request matches the Access-Control-Allow-Origin header and will disallow the request if the match returned a negative. In addition, it will disallow the request if the Access-Control-Allow-Origin is not found in the response.

To demonstrate, assume that client code from abc.alphabet.com will send this request for a resource at preschool.school.com:

```
GET /greeting/ HTTP/1.1
User-Agent: Mozilla/5.0 (Macintosh; Intel Mac OS X 10_8_5) AppleWebKit/536.30.1
(KHTML, like Gecko) Version/6.0.5 Safari/536.30.1
Accept: application/json, text/plain, */*
Referer: http://abc.alphabet.com/
Origin: http://abc.alphabet.com
```

The Origin header indicates to the server that the origin of the client code is http://abc.alphabet.com. As the request complies with the same-origin policy, the server decides that it can serve the request. The response may look like the following:

```
HTTP/1.1 200 OK
Content-Type: application/json;charset=UTF-8
Date: Tue, 01 Aug 2017 20:35:00 GMT
Server: Apache-Coyote/1.1
Content-Length: 35
Connection: keep-alive
Access-Control-Allow-Origin: http://abc.alphabet.com

[response payload]
```

The Access-Control-Allow-Origin header of the response allows access to "http://abc.alphabet.com and disallows access to all other origins.

In some cases, the Access-Control-Allow-Origin can be set to "*" to allow access to all client origins. This practice is generally considered unsafe except when an API is public and intended for consumption by any client.

Pre-flight Requests

A simple request may be insufficient if there are implications on user data. In such cases, a preflight CORS request needs to be sent ahead of the actual request to ensure that it will be safe to send the actual request.

A preflight request is warranted when the actual request uses an HTTP method other than POST, GET, or HEAD or in cases where the content type of a POST request is not one of the white-listed types. For instance, if a POST request comes with an entity body with application/json as its Content-Type, you'll need to send a preflight request. A preflight request is also necessary if the request uses custom headers.

A preflight request uses the OPTIONS method to obtain vital information from the server. The method asks the remote server for a list of methods and headers that can be sent along with the request to the specified resource.

To illustrate, assume that a client code served from abc.alphabet.com is set to perform a DELETE request on a resource at preschool.school.com. The preflight request can use the OPTIONS method using these headers:

```
OPTIONS/resource/12345
User-Agent: Mozilla/5.0 (Macintosh; Intel Mac OS X 10_8_5) AppleWebKit/536.30.1
(KHTML, like Gecko) Version/6.0.5 Safari/536.30.1
Access-Control-Request-Method: DELETE
Access-Control-Request-Headers: origin, x-requested-with, accept
Origin: http://abc.alpabet.com
```

Essentially, the above request is asking the server if the DELETE request would be allowed. If the server allows the request as outlined, it will send the response to the preflight request. The response can be similar to this:

```
HTTP/1.1 200 OK
Date: Wed, 20 Nov 2013 19:36:00 GMT
Server: Apache-Coyote/1.1
Content-Length: 0
Connection: keep-alive
Access-Control-Allow-Origin: http://abc.alphabet.com
Access-Control-Allow-Methods: POST, GET, OPTIONS, DELETE
Access-Control-Max-Age: 86400
```

Based on the values returned for the Access-Control-Allow-Methods, the response indicates that the server allows the client to issue a DELETE request against the specified resource. The value provided for the Access-Control-Max-Age states that the response is valid for 86,400 seconds or one day. Beyond this, the client must issue a new preflight request.

Resource Sharing Check

The server uses the configured headers as a mechanism to facilitate communication with the user-agent. They do not provide any assurance that a source origin will be able to override the same-origin policy.

Since the user-agent has control over the SOP, it is responsible for determining if the source origin and the Access-Control-Allow-Origin header value are in compliance with the authorization requirements.

The user-agent does this by performing these steps:

- If the response indicates zero or two or more Access-Control-Allow-Origin values, return fail and end the algorithm.
- If the Access-Control-Allow-Origin header's value set to the * character, return fail and end this algorithm.
- If the Access-Control-Allow-Origin header's value is not a case-sensitive match against the Origin header's value as specified, return fail and end the algorithm.
- If the omit credentials tag is not set and the Access-Control-Allow-Credentials header of the response contains zero or two or more values, return fail and end this algorithm.
- If the omit credentials tag is not set and the value of the Access-Control-Allow-Credentials header is not a case-sensitive match for 'true', return fail and end this algorithm.

6. Return pass.

To put it simply, the server-configured value of the Access-Control-Allow-Origin should satisfy all origins by through the wild card * token or be supplied as a case-sensitive match for the specified origin.

If the resource-sharing test result indicates that the request should not be authorized, the user-agent will raise a network error stating that the origin does not have sufficient authorization.

The following example uses PHP to demonstrate how a resource can properly authorize all source origins:

```
<?php
header('Access-Control-Allow-Origin: *');
$headers=getallheaders();
$origin =$headers["Origin"];
echo '{"message":"congratulations'.$origin.', your
origin has been successfully authorized by your
user-agent"}';
?>
```

Notice how the wild card token was assigned to the Access-Control-Allow-Origin header. At the very least, the server should set this configuration for the said header to allow all origins to be granted authorization.

Using the CORS Options and Access-Control-Allow-Origin headers, you can successfully sidestep the SOP and allow cross-origin request. This, however, does not mean that a cross-origin request will be accorded the same treatment given to an SOP-compliant request.

Although the cross-origin request has been authorized by the server, the browser will still refrain from supplying data that may compromise the security of the response or the client. Hence, custom headers, basic, authorization, and cookies are not allowed to reach their destination unless there was coordination between the server and the user-agent.

In addition, the browser will restrict the application's exposure to server-provided headers that are not included in the list of acceptable simple response headers.

Here are the white-listed response headers:

Content-Type

Content-Language

Cache-Control

Pragma

Last-Modified

Expires

To widen the scope of authorization and enable the aspects required by an application, the server need to communicate with the browser by setting the required headers as specified by CORS.

While CORS is the official W3C mechanism for handling cross-origin requests, bear in mind that the headers specified in CORS can only be utilized by browsers that comply with its algorithms. In other words, browsers that enforce XMLHttpRequest level 2 are the only user-agents that can fully implement cross-origin resource sharing.

The two other techniques that enable CORS are Proxy and JSONP.

The Proxy

While it was mentioned earlier that it is the browser that implements the same-origin polity, SOP is simply a security model enforced by browsers and it is not part of the HTTP protocol. HTTP protocol depends on the server's ability to fulfill a request. The targeted server is responsible for assessing if the request should be authorized.

A server proxy is one that transmits an authorized request to a remote server. The process starts when an HTTP request is submitted to a web server of the same origin. From that point, the local web server sends the same or a new request to a remote web server. This happens without the intervention of the browser. Assuming that the request was successful, the response is returned from the remote server to the local server that sent the request and back to the client that invoked the request.

Following is an example of an HTTP Request to the authorized/ proxy.php resource:

```
var xhr= new XMLHttpRequest();
xhr.open("GET","http://abc.alphabet.com/proxy.php");
xhr.onload=function(){
console.log(this.responseText);
};
xhr.onerror=function(){
console.log( "Error Occurred" );
}
xhr.send();
```

Once the request has been submitted, the target of the request will be executed. In the above example, the target is local resource/ proxy.php.

The following example demonstrates the server-side implementation of Proxy:

```
<?php
if ($_SERVER['REQUEST_METHOD'] === 'GET') {
$ch = curl_init();
curl_setopt($ch,
CURLOPT_URL,'http://abc.alphabet.com/chapter4/data/images.json').
curl_setopt($ch, CURLOPT_RETURNTRANSFER, false);
$output = curl_exec($ch);
curl_close($ch);
}
?>
```

The script starts by ensuring that the GET method is specified on proxy.php. This prevents the proxy from taking other requests other than GET.

The next line initializes the cURL object which, in turn, will return an instance which is stored in a variable called $ch. As with xhr object, the instance of the cURL object is configured with the required headers/values to initiate the request.

The next line supplies the URL of the resource, namely "http://abc.alphabet.com/chapter4/data/images.json"

The subsequent line configures the response to be a string instead of returning it directly. The value was set to false as there's no need to change the response from the remote server.

The next line is used to execute the request: $output = curl_exec($ch).

Finally, once the response is obtained, the cURL resource is closed.

JSONP

The last technique that you can use to interchange JSON between two different origins is JSON with padding, also called JSONP. This technique allows a client to obtain JSON through the <script> element of HTML.

The SOP has no control on requests for externally referenced data through specific HTML tags. The tags are <iframe>, <script>m <style>, <img>. Script tags are capable of embedding externally referenced JavaScript files regardless of their origins.

The following script targets the jQuery Script, an externally-hosted script, from a Content Delivery Network (CDN):

```
<script src="//code.jquery.com/jquery-1.11.0.min.js">
</script>
```

The above example retrieves the jQuery library from the jQuery CDN using the <script> tag. Once this is obtained, the jQuery Script will have full access to the current document and the document will have access to the JQuery library. This is an ideal transport for JSON. Take note, however, that some JSON value can't be properly parsed when retrieved through the <script> element.

The following example illustrates a valid JSON used as the content of a specified resource found at the http:// json.alphabet.com/chapter5/data/imagesXYZ.json:

```
{
images: [
{
title: "Image One",
url: "img/people.jpg"
}, {
title: "Image Two",
url: "img/TSQL.jpg"
}, {
title: "Image Three",
url: "img/php.jpg"
}, {
title: "Image Three",
url: "img/Rails.jpg"
}
]
}
```

Like the previous example on the inclusion of jQuery into a document, you can easily load imagesXYZ.json to an application as an external reference through the script tag:

```
<script
src="http://json.alphabet.com/chapter5/data/imagesXYZ.json">
</script>
```

However, if you try to include this code in an HTML, you'll get a syntax error of 'Uncaught SyntaxError: Unexpected token' when you view the document in the browser. This error stems from the way the script engine reads JavaScript. The supplied content is not a valid JavaScript and this caused the syntax error.

The ECMA-262 standardization rules on Expression Statements states the following:

> An ExpressionStatement cannot start with an opening curly brace because that might make it ambiguous with a Block.

In other words, the parser threw the syntax error because of the initial braces.

To go about this restriction, you'll have to convince the browser to evaluate the supplied content as an expression.

JavaScript provides the grouping operator indicated by the open and close parenthetical (( )) tokens to manage this situation. You can use the grouping operator to wrap the script and thus tell the parser to evaluate the script as an expression. The use of the parentheses to pad the expression is the reason why this technique is called JSON with padding. Once this is done, the script engine should be able to parse the content successfully.

To obtain the parsed data, you can take advantage of the JSONP model. You will need to precede JSONP with a function name which will be called when the script is evaluated. The function, in this case, acts as an event handler. The object literal will be parsed into a JavaScript object and supplied as the argument for the function. This allows the function to retrieve the parsed JSON.

Here's the syntax for JSONP:

```
CALLBACK_IDENTIFIER( JSONtext );.
```

Here's an example of the JSONP model:

```
myMethod({ "letters" : "abc" });
```

Take note that the HTML document should include a function with the same name as that of the function prepended to the JSONP. Otherwise, the parser will throw a ReferenceError.

Chapter Summary

- All browsers implement the same-origin policy (SOP).
- The SOP restricts network access between varying origins.
- The SOP manages various front-end securities.
- The level of implementation of SOP varies among different technologies.
- Cross-network errors can be rectified by enabling CORS or transferring the resource to the same domain as that of the source origin.

- A domain and its subdomain are not considered automatically authorized.
- Origins are considered similar if they have similar domain, port, and scheme.
- The port address for HTTP is 80.
- The port address for HTTPS is 443.
- The setRequestHeader cannot be used to alter certain headers.
- SOPs can be sidestepped using server-side programming.
- The Access-Control-Allow-Origin header is needed to carry out simple cross-origin request.
- A request that is not classified as "simple" requires "preflight".
- A "simple" request use POST, GET, or HEAD and is limited to four headers.
- The Content-Type header of a simple request can only be set as text/plain, mutipart/form-data, or application/x-www-form-urlencoded.
- CORS headers may only be used with browsers that comply with the algorithms of CORS specification.
- JSONP refers to JSON wrapped in parenthetical token with a prepended function name.
- The request indicates the name of the function through the jsonp query parameter.
- The SOP has no control over requests of externally referenced content using the <script> tag.
- An ExpressionStatement should not begin with an opening curly brace.
- A server proxy transfers a previously authorized request to a remote server.

CHAPTER 9: POSTING JSON

As you may have realized, a server is capable of providing a tailored response that will best conform to the configured headers, specified method, and resource of a request.

Combined with static content, this protocol can be used by the server software to convert a request into a location for the said resource. The resource's defined path is translated into a directory through the server. The response can be the file's content or a 404 message.

REQUEST ENTITY BODY

HTTP request methods are categorized into safe and unsafe methods. To put it simply, a safe method only retrieves a resource while an unsafe method seeks to supply data with an HTTP request. The resource is referred to as payload. The payload can be a simple one like an e-mail address and can be as complex as a file. Once the data is received, it is usually posted to a database for retrieval.

The resource entity, however, will have little to no use if not for the server-side code that receives and processes the incoming payload. Once handled properly, it can be very powerful.

To retrieve the payload of an IncomingMessage object, you have to consume it using the stream object's inherited interface. This can be done by attaching an event listener to the instance of the incoming request. The goal is to enable the monitoring of the stream for the data payload. Additionally, you can consume pieces of data from the stream while it is being received by using the listener with a callback that can accommodate incremental data as argument.

Here's the code:

```
function requestHandler(request, response) {
request.addListener('data', function(chunk) {
});
//...truncated
```

The application may start utilizing every piece of incoming data depending on whether the payload is in ASCII or binary. Moreover, by keeping tab of the end event of the stream, the application can be alerted when stream data has been exhausted.

You will use this code to monitor the end event:

```
function requestHandler(request, response) {
//...truncated
request.addListener(end, function() {
// stream no longer has data
});
}
```

You will need the above codes to retrieve an entity body from a request. The codes' implementation within the body will ultimately depend on the application's requirements. For instance, you will set how the chunks of data will be consumed (whether accumulated or immediately parsed) based on data expectancies and the application's needs.

Additionally, the method used to parse the data is completely dependent on the incoming payload's Content-Type. A GET request, for instance, will only supply data in URL-encoded format. A POST request, on the other hand, is capable of providing data in different formats such as text/xml, application/x-www-form-urlencoded, multipart/form-data, application/json, and so much more.

HTML Form POST

The HTML <form> element is a common way for users to provide data through a variety of syntactical components like radio buttons, check boxes, or input fields to a web application. It is used to POST data to servers.

In order to illustrate how a form POST is executed, you'll have to create the HTML document that the application can return as a resource. Following is the HTML markup that will be supplied to incoming requests:

```
<!doctype html>
<html lang="en">
<head>
    <meta charset="utf-8">
</head>
<body>
    <form action="formPost" method="POST" content="application/x-wwwform-
    urlencoded">
    First Name: <input name="fname" type="text" size="22"/>
    Last Name: <input name="lname" type="text" size="22"/>
    <input type="submit"/>
    </form>
</body>
</html>
```

You'll notice that the above is a standard HTML code. There are five lines that refer to the form within the <body> tag.

The HTML <form> element declares the container that will contain the form elements. It is likewise used to set the primary aspects of a request.

The 'action' attribute specifies the target resource of the method. In the above code, the resource specified was 'formPOST. The 'method' attribute was specified as POST. Together, the 'action' and 'method' attributes will be used to create the HTTP request line.

The 'content' attribute specifies the Content-Type of the data that will come with the request. Take note that there are only three Content-Type values that can be used in an HTML form: text/plain, multipart/form-data, and application/x-www-form-urlencoded. If the content attribute was not specified on the form, the Content-Type will be set to application/x-www-form-urlencoded by default.

The succeeding lines specify the input fields that will capture individual data. The 'name' attribute is used to define the key that will be used to convey the given value. The keys in this example are 'fname' and 'lname' which correspond to the user's First Name and Last Name, respectively. The 'text' value was assigned to the 'type' attribute and a corresponding 'size' was provided.

Finally, the code uses another input field to create a 'Submit' button. Providing the submit value to the input type attribute specifies the input field as a button. The submit button is used to invoke data submission. The form initiates the request when a user clicks on the button.

Processing a JSON POST

Forms allow websites to gather data supplied by its users. However, the Content-Types provided by forms do not support JSON structure. To send JSON, you will need to configure an XMLHttpRequest object.

You can apply your knowledge of AJAX to enable the HTML form to process JSON. You may add the following to the mark-up code:

```
<script>
function ajax() {
  var xhr = new XMLHttpRequest();
  xhr.open("POST", "formPost");
  xhr.setRequestHeader("Content-Type",
  "application/json");
  var input = document.getElementsByTagName("input");
  var obj = {
    fname : input[0].value,
    lname : input[1].value
  };
  xhr.send(JSON.stringify(obj));
return false;
}
</script>
```

CHAPTER 10: WORKING WITH TEMPLATES

A template is at tool for implementing structure and providing consistency among interchangeable parts. Templates allow interchangeable parts to be used indistinguishably within a structure. Templates offer flexibility which makes them a reliable tool in website development.

Currently, there are many platforms that rely on templates and this has led to the popularity of content management systems (CMS) like WordPress and Drupal. These platforms typically utilize server-side programming to inject database content. With the advent of AJAX, however, templates soon weaved their way to front-end programming. Currently, there are several templating engines that can be used including Moustache, Handlebars, and JSRender, and Dust. These engines depend on JSON.

Handlebars

Handlebars is a JavaScript templating agent that uses its own syntax to achieve the required templating behavior. It offers a more elegant templating system than what you would get by using JavaScript to define your templates. Handlebars templates employ the same semantic tags as that used in HTML.

Installation

Before you can use the Handlebars library, you will need to obtain the latest source code from the http://handlebarsjs.com website. The quickest way is to manually download the source code by clicking on the orange button with a "Download 4.0.10" label. The latest version is 4.0.10.

Once it has completed downloading, you can save the file in a more appropriate folder.

Now that you have downloaded the Handlebars library, you can incorporate it within your HTML document through the <script> element.

The following snippet includes the Handlebars version 4.0.10 into the <head?> section of a page using the <script> tag.

```
<head>
<script src="js/libs/handlebars-v4.0.10.js"></script>
</head>
```

You may choose not to download the library and simply include a reference to a CDNJS library. Handlebars is hosted on several CDNs.

Here's an example:

```
https://cdnjs.cloudflare.com/ajax/libs/handlebars.js/4.0.10/handlebars.amd.js
```

Working with Handlebars

A Handlebars expression is marked by two pairs of opening and closing curly braces like the following example:

```
<h1>{{title}}</h1>
```

Placeholder - a Basic Expression

A basic expression consists of a reference to a key which is wrapped inside two curly braces like the above example. It is more commonly referred to as a placeholder due to the fact that at runtime, it is expected to be replaced by the value of a key-value pair stored in a collection in which a member matches the given key.

A placeholder is the most basic Handlebars expression. You can use it to replace static elements like numbers and/or strings.

The following example demonstrates the most basic way to use Handlebars template:

```
<!DOCTYPE html>
<html lang="en">
<head>
<meta charset="utf-8">
<script src="js/libs/handlebars-v4.0.10.js"></script>
</head>
<body>
<script type="application/x-handlebars" id="Handlebar-
Name-Template">
<span> {{name}} </span>
</script>
<script type="application/javascript">
var initialTemplateWrapper
= document.getElementById("Handlebar-Name-Template");
var initialTemplateContent
= initialTemplateWrapper.innerHTML;
var dynamicTempate
= Handlebars.compile(initialTemplateContent);
var markupOutput = dynamicTempate({ "name" : "Justine" });
document.getElementsByTagName("body")[0].innerHTML
= markupOutput;
</script>
</body>
</html>
```

Defining a Handlebars Template

Defining a Handlebars template involves designing a semantic layout with HTML elements and specifying a basic expression. To illustrate, here is an example of a simple template with a single placeholder:

```
<!DOCTYPE html>
<html lang="en">
<head>
<meta charset="utf-8">
<script src="js/libs/handlebars-v4.0.10.js"></script>
</head>
<body>
<script type="text/x-handlebars-template"
id="Handlebar-Name-Template">
<span class="name">{{name}}<span>
</script>
</body>
</html>
```

The above example starts like any other HTML document. The difference lies in the inclusion of the Handlebars library. The <script> element is used to load the external Handlebars library into the document. This will allow the document to utilize its templating engine.

The code for the Handlebars template is found within the surrounding <script> tags. Based on the script tag's type attribute, the template is not JavaScript. Instead, the script tag is specified as a text type. Specifically, this subset of text is used to define a Handlebars template.

This template specifies a single placeholder which is stored within the <span> tags. The basic expression is surrounded by two pairs of curly braces within the template. In JavaScript, an expression refers to the evaluation and return of data. In this example, the {{name}} is the basic expression that will be replaced with a value to be retained by a member that will match the expression. In addition, each time a reference is made to this template, you can expect that it will generate a span tag with an arbitrary name.

If you run the code, the result will be a blank document. This can be traced to the fact that the document does not contain an HTML markup for rendering. The template doesn't render because of the <script> tag around it.

The Impact of the <script> tag

There are several reasons why you should wrap a template within the script tag.

The script tag prevents the template from being rendered and hides the placeholder from the visitor's view. The W3C specifications state that script tags will not be rendered as they will have to be provided to appropriate script engine for evaluation.

However, you don't really want to supply your template to a script engine for parsing. Hence, the type attribute needs to be set to a scripting language that is unrecognizable to the browser. In the above example, the scripting language provided was text/ x-handlebars-template.

By specifying that the script holds a Handlebars template, you're inhibiting the browser from sending the template to a script engine. In addition, it allows other developers to quickly recognize the content as a Handlebars template.

When you specify the template within the <script> tag, you are actually creating an inline template. Associating the template within the same document that will be using it can confer tremendous benefits in terms of maintainability.

Lastly, as with other elements, using the <script> element allows us to refer to the template through a specific ID. This is extremely important as you will need this association to utilize the template.

Compiling a Template

In the previous example, you learned to define a basic template. The template, as you may have realized, has no impact at all on the document. For the template to work, you'll need to supply it to the Handlebars library for it to be compiled into a JavaScript function.

To accomplish this, you'll need to supply the content for the ID Handlebar-Name-Template to the Handlebars object method. This can be achieved by adding five more lines to the current code as demonstrated by the following example:

```
</script>
<script type="application/javascript">
var templateWrapper = document.getElementById("Handlebar-Name-Template");
var templateContent = templateWrapper.innerHTML;
var tempateFunction = Handlebars.compile(templateContent);
</script>
```

The above snippet shows the lines of code that will be used to convert the template into a function that you can call repeatedly and supply with a JSON argument.

The first line of the snippet indicates that you'll need JavaScript to compile the template.

The second line targets the template that you want to compile. Applying the getElementById method and supplying the Handlebar-Name-Template associates the script to the script element that holds the template. The returned element was assigned to a variable named templateWrapper.

The next line uses the innerHTML property to extract the text found between the opening and closing <script> tag and assigns the returned value to a variable named templateContent.

The next step supplies the templateContent as an argument to the compile method of the Handlebars object.

Providing Context to a Template

Providing a template as an argument to the compile method will cause it to return a JavaScript function. Assigning this function to a variable will allow you to repeatedly call the function. When called, this function will take a JSON argument.

Here is the syntax for the template function:

function(object);

The object supplied to the template function is called context in Handlebars terminology mainly because it represents the data set or model that provides value to placeholders or Handlebars expressions.

To demonstrate how you can use a compiled template to render JSON data to an HTML document, you can add the two lines of code below within the script tag of your existing markup:

```
var outputMarkup = templateFunction( { "name":"Jayson" } );
alert( outputMarkup );
```

The first line calls the templateFunction and provides a JSON object with one key-value pair. Notice that the key used in the JSON data matches the label of the placeholder for the template.

The template works by replacing the label for the placeholder with the corresponding value of a key with the same name if it occurs on the supplied context. In this case, the placeholder label was 'name' which was also the label of the key in the supplied JSON data.

When you compile a template through Handlebars.compile, the template is converted into a JavaScript function. Whenever you call the function and supply JSON data, the function is implemented by assigning JSON values to the placeholders and returning a string.

The second line is used to alert users to the result.

In the above example, you have invoked the template function by supplying one key-value pair. You can provide varying contexts with each function call to generate varying output.

Here's an example:

```
var outputMarkup;
outputMarkup = templateFunction( { "name":"Jayson" } );
console.log( outputMarkup ); // <span> Jayson </span>
outputMarkup = templateFunction( { "name":"Cole" } );
console.log( outputMarkup ); // <span> Cole </span>
outputMarkup = templateFunction( { "name":"Job" } );
console.log( outputMarkup ); // <span> Job</span>
```

Multiple Placeholders

A template can consist of more than one placeholder. The following snippet demonstrates how you can achieve it:

```
//..truncated code
<body>
<section id="directory">
<script type="application/x-handlebars" id="Handlebar-Student-Template">
<div class="student">
<p> firstName: {{fName}} </p>
<p> lastName: {{lName}} </p>
<p> age: {{age}} </p>
</div>
</script>
</section>
<script>
</script>
</body>
```

The above code defines a template named Handlebar-Student-Template. This template will contain the first name, last name, and age within the individual paragraph element. The three paragraphs are contained within a <div> tag with 'student' as the class attribute's value.

Chapter Summary

- Handlebars is a templating engine.
- Handlebars templates wrapped as a string inside <script> tags.
- The script type is provided as an unidentifiable language to prevent the template from being supplied to and parsed by JavaScript engine.
- A placeholder is the most basic expression in Handlebars.
- All expressions correspond to keys stored by JSON data.
- At runtime, a Handlebars template is converted into a JavaScript function.

CHAPTER 11: JSON WITH PHP

JSON is commonly used when data needs to be retrieved from a server and displayed in a website.

This chapter will discuss the exchange of JSON data between a PHP server and a client.

PHP uses the following built-in functions to work with JSON data:

- json_encode
- json_decode
- json_last_error

Php json_encode() function

This function is used to encode PHP objects to JSON. If successful, it returns the JSON representation of the specified value. If unsuccessful, it returns FALSE.

The following example converts a PHP object to JSON:

```
<?php
$myObj->name = "Jack";
$myObj->age = 27;
$myObj->city = "Los Angeles";

$myJSON = json_encode($myObj);

echo $myJSON;
?>
```

It will result to the following key-value pairs in JSON format:

```
{"name":"Jack","age":27,"city":"Los Angeles"}
```

PHP json_decode() function

This function is used to return the value decoded from JSON to a corresponding PHP type.

Syntax:

mixed json_decode($json [,$assoc = false [, $depth = 512 [, $options = 0]]])

Parameters:

json_string The string must be a UTF-8 encoded data.

assoc This is a Boolean-type parameter. When set to TRUE, it converts returned objects into associative arrays.

depth This integer-type parameter is used to specify recursion depth.

options This parameter is an integer-type bitmask for JSON. It supports JSON_BIGINT_AS_STRING.

The following code demonstrates how you can use PHP to decode JSON objects:

```
<html>
   <body>
         <?php
         $json = '{"x":1,"y":2,"z":3}';

         var_dump(json_decode($json));
         var_dump(json_decode($json, true));
         print "var_dump";
      ?>
   </body>
</html>
```

Here's what the result might be:

```
object(stdClass)#1 (3) { ["x"]=> int(1) ["y"]=> int(2) ["z"]=> int(3) }
array(3) { ["x"]=> int(1) ["y"]=> int(2) ["z"]=> int(3) }var_dump
```

Conclusion:

Thank you for downloading and reading this book. You have just learned a valuable web development tool that can help you grow and flourish as a web application developer. I hope that this special skill will help you achieve your personal and career objectives.

Did you enjoy this book?

We want to thank you for purchasing and reading this book. We really hope you got a lot out of it.

Thanks so much.
iCode Academy

www.ingramcontent.com/pod-product-compliance
Ingram Content Group UK Ltd.
Pitfield, Milton Keynes, MK11 3LW, UK
UKHW040654040325
4843UKWH00038B/523

9 781393 048671